THE
CONCISE

Guide to Telephone Tactics

Graham Roberts-Phelps

THORO**g**OOD

Published by Thorogood
10-12 Rivington Street
London EC2A 3DU

Telephone: 020 7749 4748
Fax: 020 7729 6110
Email: info@thorogood.ws
Web: www.thorogood.ws

A CIP catalogue record for this book is
available from the British Library.

ISBN 1 85418 278 1

Designed and typeset by Driftdesign.

Printed in India by Replika Press.

About the author

Graham Roberts-Phelps

Graham Roberts-Phelps is an international specialist consultant in business and personal development, sharing his ideas and insights with thousands of people and organisations every year. With an extensive background in management and business development, Graham works with organisations of many different types and sizes, as a professional trainer and consultant.

Introduction

My purpose in writing this book, is to provide you with a practical handbook on using the telephone to improve your business.

Whether your focus is customer satisfaction, gaining sales, making appointments, or simply to communicate with colleagues more efficiently, I am sure you can glean some new tips and techniques. You may find that you remember a few old, and perhaps forgotten, skills and ideas too.

Good luck.
Graham Roberts-Phelps

Look out for these!

Take a tip...

Throughout the book **handy tips** relevant to the particular subject matter will be displayed in the quote marks featured.

Draw on your initiative!

A pen or pencil will be useful when you complete numerous questionnaires, action plans and tests.

These are extremely *useful tips* to remember while you are conducting, or planning a telephone call!

Contents

PART ONE
TELEPHONE TACTICS FOR CUSTOMER SATISFACTION   1

The telecommunications revolution   2

Creating a positive impression   4

Master the basics   10

Effective telephone guidelines   16

Helpful words and phrases   21

Advanced telephone rapport   31

Structuring a telephone call   34

Telephone skills assessment   38

Gathering information – key skills   43

Turning customer problems into opportunities   45

Confirming – key skills   50

Difficult situations – key skills   51

Dealing with angry customers   55

Assertiveness on the telephone   60

Attitude   63

Telephone skills – best practise summary   65

Customer service – application assignments   67

PART TWO
GAINING APPOINTMENTS BY TELEPHONE

69

The importance of proactive prospecting 70

Sales is a numbers game 72

The most important step in the sales process 77

Ten top tips on making appointments 79

Making appointments: planning and preparation 83

Getting past gatekeepers 91

How to structure a call 97

Cold-calling blues 104

'Warm-calling': A three-step method
to increase your sales 108

Ideal appointment times 118

Example call 119

Prospect tracking 121

Appointments – application assignments 124

PART THREE
ACHIEVING BETTER SALES RESULTS ON THE TELEPHONE 125

How to get even better sales results	126
Customer focus	129
Selling and customer service	131
An introduction to selling on the telephone	132
Structuring a sales call	137
Preparation, organisation and planning	140
Converting incoming calls into sales	145
Outgoing calls – working a list	148
Personal organisation	152
Activities levels	154
Voice projection	158
The sales call	160
The voice that sells	161
Telephone sales questioning techniques	163
Features and benefits (FAB)	176
Developing FAB statements	178
People buy for different reasons	180
Handling objections and questions	183
Overcoming objections	186
Closing the sale	189
Ending the call	193
Telephone selling – application assignments	195

PART ONE

TELEPHONE TACTICS FOR CUSTOMER SATISFACTION

The telecommunications revolution	2
Creating a positive impression	4
Master the basics	10
Effective telephone guidelines	16
Helpful words and phrases	21
Advanced telephone rapport	31
Structuring a telephone call	34
Telephone skills assessment	38
Gathering information – key skills	43
Turning customer problems into opportunities	45
Confirming – key skills	50
Difficult situations – key skills	51
Dealing with angry customers	55
Assertiveness on the telephone	60
Attitude	63
Telephone skills – best practise summary	65
Customer service – application assignments	67

TELEPHONE TACTICS FOR CUSTOMER SATISFACTION

The telecommunications revolution

We are in the midst of what experts call 'the telecommunications revolution'. Just as the development of the four stroke engine and the production line system revolutionised industry earlier this century, so telecommunications involving the merger of computer and telephone technology is doing so now.

Many industries such as the financial services and banking sectors, have already seen a revolution in dealing with customers over the telephone. Telephones are also very important in helping businesses to retain customers, and in particular, to keep them happy – that is, if we are able to use the telephone correctly!

Telephones offer us tremendous advantages as well. They are a fast, efficient and an effective method of communication. We can speak to as many people in a few minutes on the telephone as we might see all day in face-to-face meetings.

They also make organisations work. Many organisations today are extremely complex, with divisions and departments spread over many different areas. A telephone can link them all instantly and effortlessly. Love them or hate them, telephones are here to stay, and getting on with others means using them well.

As the telephone is so widely used in business, indeed it may be our major (or in some cases only) contact with customers, it is vitally important that we excel in all areas of telephone communications.

It is also important to remember its effect in helping our company or organisation to run more efficiently. A great deal of our internal communication (that is with our colleagues), indeed some of our most important communication, is effected over the telephone.

The great telephone challenge

Your goal when using the telephone for internal or external customers should be to:

- make that caller believe that you are pleased to hear from them
- sound awake, alert and ready
- make the caller feel special
- have patience with those who perhaps deserve it the least
- direct your personality and enthusiasm down the telephone
- make a good first impression
- make a good last impression
- keep in control, without interrupting or bullying
- inspire confidence
- make the customer feel they are dealing with a person and not being processed
- not use any negative words or phrases
- be believed
- use the customer's name regularly
- conduct the call efficiently and quickly without rushing the caller.

That's all!

Creating a positive impression

Have you ever spoken to someone on the telephone before meeting them – were they what you expected?

When we communicate on the telephone, we are attempting to transfer an image from our mind to the minds of our listeners. To do this, we need to speak and select words with which we describe our mental image or ideas and thoughts.

Customers create an impression of you and your company based on how you sound.

When our listeners hear our words, they form a mental picture of what we are trying to convey through these words. However, people don't always have the same meaning for a given voice tone, word or phrase and so we have communication breakdowns. For example, we could say 'No thank you' to mean several things, and depending on how we say it – even 'YES!'

As with face-to-face contact, telephone communication provides an exchange of views and some form of feedback on our presentation. However, there are some important differences between telephone communication and face-to-face contact. Understanding these differences is crucial to success in using this medium.

Non-verbal communications

In normal communication the make-up of communications is:

content 7%

voice 38%

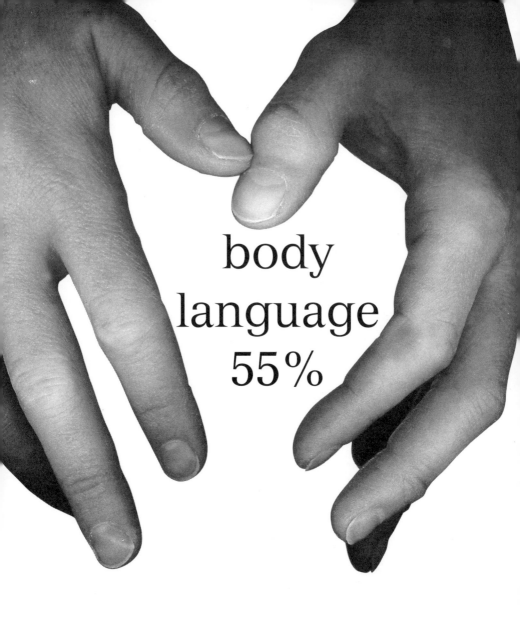

body
language
55%

This is why paying attention to what people *do*, rather than what they *say*, can be so effective. There is 13 times more information available in non-verbal communication than in words.

On the telephone, however, the visual communication element is imagined or visualised in the mind's-eye by the brain in order to compensate.

Reduced feedback

Perhaps the most significant difference about being on the telephone is that you are cut off from your normal sources of feedback or communication. In a face-to-face situation, you can rely on a number of visual clues – facial expressions, body postures, gestures – to gauge the other person's reaction to your message, but these are not available to you over the telephone.

This means that when you are communicating over the telephone, all you have to go on are those clues provided by the other person's voice, for example:

- tone of voice
- volume
- speech rate
- the actual words.

LIMITATIONS DUE TO REDUCED FEEDBACK

The fact is that without visual clues, you are more likely to **misinterpret** statements.

- Being limited to voice clues, you will need a high degree of **concentration**
- Conversations may become too **impersonal** and **businesslike**

- Time tends to become **exaggerated** (ie 20 seconds waiting on the telephone can seem much longer)

- Not knowing what the customer may be doing, you may **interrupt** them at an inopportune moment.

Quick solutions to common difficulties

MISINTERPRETATION

Use of 'active' listening skills can help you avoid misinterpreting customer statements.

DISEMBODIED VOICE

Get to know the speaker as a person – when they engage in personal conversation, let them do it – you'll learn more about them that way.

DESK-TIED

Organise your desk so that everything you need is within reach and you have no need to leave your telephone to gather information or support material.

EXAGGERATE TIME

Exaggerated time is primarily a matter of not leaving the other person on 'hold' for excessive amounts of time. Also, be reasonably direct and to the point.

INTERRUPTING CUSTOMERS

If you interrupt a customer who is very busy and doesn't want to talk when you ring, it's best to re-schedule the call. You can also try to establish a convenient time to call.

Master the basics

People like people who sound...

People like to deal with people who have a certain 'attitude' or charisma about them. This is true whether you are dealing face-to-face, or on the telephone. If we don't have any face-to-face or visual communication, we have to use our voice to create the right impression. Most people would agree that they would like to be described by their customers as:

- friendly
- helpful
- cheerful
- knowledgeable
- confident
- in control
- professional
- enthusiastic
- organised
- awake
- sexy (!)
- in charge.

Tick two words from the list above that would fit your approach, or add those you would rather use.

These are all words that we would like to create in the mind of our customer, or the person we are dealing with on the other end of the telephone. There is no great difficulty in doing this, so long as we are able to take control of our own physiology and verbal behaviours. The most important thing to understand is that we only have our voice to do this with, and it is voice tone that people interpret and use to judge us.

How to create a positive physiology

SMILE WHILE YOU DIAL

It is true that you can hear a smile down the telephone. And it is this smile that creates a positive, friendly, cheerful and helpful impression at the other end. We have all experienced the caller, or the person on the other end of the telephone, who sounds really fed up, and this leaves us with a very negative image.

The truth is that it is impossible to feel depressed while you are smiling. It is also true that if we met somebody face-to-face, nine times out of ten we would want to smile, or at least have them smile at us. The telephone is no different. So make sure that you put a smile on your face whenever you are on the telephone.

POSTURE

The next thing that will help you create a good impression is to sit up straight; in some cases it may even help to stand up. Not only will this help you feel more confident, you will also find that your voice will sound different. Whilst the customer or the caller may not know that you are standing up, they will intuitively sense the difference in your voice and approach. This is because our diaphragm is actually larger and more open when we are standing or sitting up straight. We will also act, and therefore sound, more alert and confident.

STAY FOCUSED

One of the most common mistakes that people make on the telephone is to allow themselves to be distracted by other people around them. The reason this is so easy to do is because we are distracted by the lack of visual communication on the telephone.

In particular, making eye contact with somebody else in the office splits our attention and makes it very difficult for us to concentrate on listening to somebody on the telephone. Therefore be careful to avoid secondary eye contact with people around you. Making notes obviously helps this, but also position yourself and your desk away from the normal sight line of people passing by or coming into your office.

REMEMBER

- Smile while you dial

- Keep an upright posture

- Avoid distractions – stay focused.

How to change your voice

When we use the telephone there are several voice techniques that we need to adopt in order to be more effective in our communication. These techniques are partly to do with the mechanics of the telephone, in that it is not a particularly high technology piece of audio equipment, and therefore our voice can get distorted or reduced.

It is also to do with the fact that because of the dynamics of the telephone (ie less visual communication), many people translate words into images, and look behind the meaning, which we would normally gain from visual, facial or body language.

Following are some of the keys to changing your voice and making it more effective over the telephone.

SPEECH RATE

The most common mistake on the telephone today is people talking too quickly.

By speaking slower, we make it easier for people to understand us. We also give our words more impact and allow ourselves slightly more time to think. The best way to change your voice is to slow it down by at least 20 per cent, although this will depend on how you speak normally of course.

VOLUME

Match the customer's speech volume or speak slightly louder than normal face-to-face conversation.

The telephone sometimes reduces the volume of our voice, therefore it is very useful to slightly increase the speaking volume when we talk. This once again aids comprehension and ensures that our words are heard correctly. Be careful not to shout though, and be sensitive to quiet speakers.

PRONUNCIATION

How we pronounce a word becomes much more important over the telephone. This is partly because of the lack of visual communication, and also because people will read into our voice tone the meaning of the word.

For example, if someone was to say on the telephone that they are very angry, you would have to assess how angry they were by the way they said it. So be very careful, and also deliberate on how you pronounce certain words, particularly if you are trying to persuade people.

Saying a particular product has a fantastic feature, can either wash over people without any effect or jump up and grab their attention, depending on how you say it.

Speak clearly – and, if necessary, spell anything that may be unclear.

EMPHASIS

We will normally use our eyes, facial expression and body gestures to emphasise words and meaning. As the telephone doesn't allow us this visual communication, the emphasis comes through a combination of the above three factors and also our emphasis on certain words and phrases. Either by repeating them, or by leaving significant pauses, can we add greater emphasis to what we say.

Try saying the following sentence, putting greater tonal emphasis on the words in italics. Notice how the meaning changes each time.

Leave this with **me** *and I will get back to you this afternoon.*

Leave this with me and **I** *will get back to you this afternoon.*

Leave this with me and I will get back to **you** *this afternoon.*

Leave this with me and I will get back to you **this afternoon.**

TELEPHONE VOICE

Your telephone voice will have an effect on the outcome of your call, so remember the following:

Pitch	More amplification and modulation, almost sing-song or melodic
Volume	Increase by 15 per cent or match the customers
Speed	Slow down by 50 per cent or adjust to match caller's speed
Pace	Mirror or match the mood and speaking style of the caller
Words	Use short words, pronounce words carefully, spell names and figures
Sentence	Speak in 'chunks' of 10-14 words at a time, listening for the caller's acknowledgement of understanding
Emphasis	Mark out words that are important with a change of voice tone, speed or volume (louder)
Pronunciation	Beware of mispronouncing words and people's names
Mood	Match the mood of the caller and don't be overly cheerful if the situation or topic does not merit it
Facial expression	SMILE!

Effective telephone guidelines

Focus on the customer

We have used the telephone most of our lives and most of us think we use it well. There are, however, some telephone practices that work especially well in business when establishing a good relationship with your customers. Remember – the old-fashioned virtues of manners, politeness and courtesy are essential. Your most important asset in telephone work is your voice, although the following points are of importance too.

BE HELPFUL

Take time to be helpful in order to build up a good relationship and customer confidence.

Customers don't care how much you know, until they know how much you care!

CHECK UNDERSTANDING

When the customer gives information, repeat the information to make sure you've heard it correctly. When you give another person information, ask a question that requires a specific answer, not just 'yes' or 'no'. If there is any misunderstanding, always assume responsibility and let the customer know you are doing so.

You never get a second chance to make a good first impression.

BE ATTENTIVE

You can tell how your customer is reacting by concentrating on their tone of voice.

Don't just listen to the facts – tune in to how the customer is feeling – sad, mad, or glad.

BE THOROUGH

Take the time to attend to each detail, so that both you and your customer have the correct information. Don't move on to another point until you both agree to move on.

PERSONALISE

Use the customer's name frequently. Engage in side conversations; be sure, however, not to be drawn too far off the subject you are discussing.

BE COURTEOUS

Always be polite. Don't interrupt. Respond to your customer's comments. If you are not concentrating, ask the customer to repeat what they have said, do not say to yourself that you will think about it when you put the telephone down. It doesn't work. Observe the rules of common courtesy.

EXCEED EXPECTATIONS

Be a little more of 'something' than the customer expects. That 'something' might be knowledgeable, patient, helpful, friendly, polite, etc.

Ten tips to business success

You communicate your attitude, confidence and competence over the telephone. Exhibiting telephone excellence can be fun and can reap unexpected rewards. These ten tips will win you business success.

1. Use appropriate volume. Speak as if someone were two or three feet away.

2. Be clear. Speak crisply. Avoid slurring syllables or trailing off at the end of words.

3. Smile. A smile conveys sincerity and enthusiasm.

4. Speed. Your speech speed can indicate your attitude. The ideal rate is 150-160 words per minute. If you speak faster, the caller may doubt your credibility. Any slower and you may bore your listener.

5. Be expressive. Be yourself. Speak like you would to a friend.

6. Use a positive language approach. The words and phrases you use shape other people's images of you and can determine how they will react to you. Try positive phrases like, 'I'd be happy to...' rather than the negative 'I have to...'

7. Use your first and last name to identify yourself.

8. Lower your voice at the end of a sentence, especially a question. This conveys confidence and competence. Raising your voice (as in your voice going up to ask a question) conveys uncertainty. Be careful to lower your vocal tone only, and not your volume.

9. Write down ideas on how to respond. Jot down key points and ideas so that you will be able to respond effectively when you have a chance to speak.

10. Change your outgoing message daily when using voice mail or an answering device. Leave a brief professional message with today's date and when you will be returning calls.

When to answer the telephone

CALL PICK-UP

When the telephone rings, you will probably be busy with other things, such as preparing to make a call to another customer, or just putting the telephone down from the previous call. Let the telephone ring at least two complete rings, but not long enough to annoy the customer. This allows you to disconnect your thoughts and concentrate upon the incoming call.

> When the phone rings – wait until the third call – use the time to prepare yourself, empty your mind, clear your throat, get a pen and mentally log-on.

You can answer the telephone too quickly as well as too slowly.

WHEN TO HANG UP

Always hang up after the customer has done so. They may have more to say or may hear you (rudely) crash the receiver down.

NO ANSWER

The general rule is to let the telephone ring eight times, before hanging up. Remember, every second you are on hold, someone might be on hold for you.

IDENTIFY YOURSELF

Your opening remark, as well as a cheerful greeting, should always contain your name, your position within the company and, if you are initiating the call, a statement explaining the purpose of the call.

HOW LONG TO HOLD

When you are on the telephone, time can seem much longer than it actually is and so some points are worth mentioning.

- Always give the customer the choice of holding, or offer to call them back with the relevant information.

- Use the hold button if the telephone has one. Remember the receiver will carry sound even though the mouthpiece is covered.

- If your customer prefers to wait, check back every 15-20 seconds.

- If you anticipate you will be away from the telephone longer than one or two minutes, you should suggest calling the customer back.

WHEN TRANSFERRING

Explain to the customer why the call is being transferred, and to whom. If the customer does not want the call to be transferred, offer to have the person concerned call the customer back.

Helpful words and phrases

The following phrases and expressions are probably not used enough on the telephone:

- you...
- thank you for waiting
- new
- interesting
- different
- I need to ask you
- would it be possible
- I promise
- before four pm tomorrow
- I will definitely do that
- certainly
- my pleasure
- it's no trouble
- please call back if you have any questions
- the best thing I can suggest is...

DO NOT USE...

- try to
- maybe
- don't know
- not my fault/department
- not possible
- I disagree
- you're wrong
- that's not true.

Unhelpful words and phrases

The following phrases and expressions in the left-hand column are frequently used on the telephone, even though they are not very 'user friendly'. In the right column is an improved version.

EXPRESSION	BETTER ALTERNATIVE
What's the problem?	*How may I help you?*
You ought to...	*May I suggest?*
The system's down.	*That may take a moment to look up, would you like me to call you back?*
I don't know what you mean by that.	I'm sorry, please could you explain that again?
No, I can't help you.	*Let me put you through to...*
You need to talk to someone else.	*Let me put you through to...*

EXPRESSION	BETTER ALTERNATIVE
Hold, please.	*Would you mind holding or can I call you back/can I help you?*
I can't do anything about it. This is our organisation's policy.	*The reason we _____ is because _____*
What did you say?	*Sorry, I seem to have a bad line, could you repeat that please?*
I can't understand you.	*Please could your repeat that? Let me take some notes.*
I'm afraid my manager is in a meeting at the moment.	*They are not available, may I help you or take a message in the meantime?*
It's not my responsibility.	*Let me put you through to...*
We don't handle that here.	*Let me put you through to...*
You have come through to the wrong extension.	*Let me put you through to...*
I haven't a clue.	*I need to look in to this, the best thing I can do is call you back at...*
There's nothing I can do.	*I'm afraid that I can't do X, but I can do Y.*
I'd advise you to...	*May I ask you to/the best thing you can do is...*

Don't ask people to call you back!

In just the same way that you may have trained people that you can be interrupted in a face-to-face environment, you will have probably unwittingly instructed people to interrupt you by telephone.

It has been shown that when business people try to contact each other, the chances of them finding them at the end of the telephone is less then 50 per cent.

What does this mean? It means that 50 per cent of the telephone calls you make will probably result in the person:

- not being 'in'!
- having his/her calls screened
- being in a meeting
- being on the telephone themselves
- being out.

This will leave you a choice of two actions:

- for you to call them back, or
- for them to call you back.

There may be an alternative. Put the information on the fax, e-mail or leave a clear message. When you ask somebody to call you back however, what you are actually doing is creating an interruption.

The trouble is that they will probably call back at the most inconvenient point they can!

It will also catch you unprepared and very often you may forget why you asked them to call you back in the first place. This may then lead to either a wasted call or you putting them on hold while you try and find your notes or information.

AVOID DELAY AND FRUSTRATION!

Follow these steps:

- If you have to, or you feel that it is polite, leave a message that you called

- Ask the operator, or the person that answered the telephone, when the person you are calling is expected back at their desk

- Get a time, if they say that they will be back in tomorrow ask the operator what would be a good time to call

- See if they would accept certain times by offering times you could call back

- Give a reason why they can't call you – 'I shall be in a meeting...', 'travelling', or try this phrase. 'I work from an outgoing diary...' This will minimise and reduce the chance of you actually missing them again.

This approach may take a little discipline, but it works extremely well for both internal and external customers. External customers do not seem to understand why they should call you back, so they actually prefer you to call them back. It also manages their expectation.

This process will also avoid the game of 'telephone tag' that seems to take place so often. This is when you call someone and leave a message for them to call back. They then return your call only to find that you have just gone to lunch. You come back from lunch to find that they have phoned, so you call them and so it goes on.

Never, never go on hold for more than 30 seconds. It only encourages companies to do it more.

Break the chain by simply not asking people to call you back. Find out when would be the best time to contact them. Schedule this call in your diary and then you will not forget it.

Prepare for telephone calls

Preparation saves time. You would prepare for a face-to-face meeting, so why not prepare for a telephone conversation?

If, for example, you were to analyse enquiries in a customer service situation, you would probably find that most of the calls are about a small number of issues or items. You will probably hear the same questions repeated throughout the day. So, prepare answers to the most important or commonly asked questions in advance of the telephone ringing. Always make sure you have the information relating to these questions to hand.

If you have to explain the same thing over and over again, then perhaps it would be an advantage to actually write down the expression, statements or questions that you could use, making sure that it is practised, concise and understandable. Clearly you wouldn't want to read this on the telephone but by just determining it in advance you will find that your communication will be clearer and more precise.

If you are making outgoing calls, no matter what the content, prepare carefully by making sure that you have any relevant notes and files that you may require, to hand. Details of any previous telephone conversations you may have had with that person and notes on your objectives or agenda points may also be useful.

Do not be afraid to schedule exact times of when to call people. In just the same way that you would set a precise time for an appointment or a meeting, do the same for a telephone call. Log it in your diary and it will remind you to make that call.

Slow your voice down on the telephone and ALWAYS ask people to repeat numbers and important details, and then repeat it back to them. This can prevent a misunderstanding AND save time.

Take notes

One of the keys to becoming effective in what you do is to think more on paper. Whether this is in planning, jotting things down that you don't want to forget, making notes following meetings or telephone calls or confirming details in writing.

One of the disadvantages of using the telephone is that sometimes the communication is very brief and may seem a little inexact. As you go through a telephone call be sure to make notes of the key points.

This also has the benefit of helping you concentrate, making sure that your eye contact does not wander off somewhere else. At the end of the telephone conversation simply review your notes out loud with the other person, checking the details that you have written down. Always be sure to read back and double check telephone numbers, dates, times, addresses and so on.

By keeping notes in this way you can actually refer back to previous conversations and double check details that were agreed, discussed or passed on.

Replace scraps of paper and 'Post-It' notes with proper message pads and notebooks. If it saves one lost message a year it's worth it!

Make sure you summarise clearly at the end of every telephone call – people remember this the most.

Be aware of time

When you make or receive telephone calls do so with a clock in front of you, or possibly even an egg timer, to see if you can get off the telephone and finish the call before the sand runs out. Just being more aware of time passing can actually make you unconsciously come to the point quicker and explain things more concisely.

Remember – you could save up to 45 minutes a day by reducing each call by a minute. Of course you may not need to make telephone calls at all. Information can simply be passed on by fax or you may have other people to whom you can delegate telephone call-backs.

Screen calls

Here are some tips that may help you or others screen calls.

- Always ask who is calling and what it is regarding before checking to see if they are available.

- Ask the caller polite questions such as 'Will they know why you are calling?' or 'What is the purpose of your call?'

- If the call is a sales call suggest that the sales person write in the first instance and ask them to call back at a specified time. (You may find it useful to assign an hour each week where you have a 'free for all' phone-in. This is the one hour that your assistant can invite salespeople to call. You may be surprised how many people don't, given that opportunity, of course, if they do, they get put straight through.)

If you do not have an assistant or work on your own – use an answer machine as 'call screening device.' Record a new topical message daily.

- If possible redirect the call to somebody else in the office who is able to handle their enquiry.

- Try to avoid too many cliché 'they are in a meeting' type expressions. Instead, take control of the call by saying 'I cannot put you through, they are not available at the moment, can I take your number and pass the details on to them?'

- Do not make promises that may not be kept. Use expressions such as 'I will ask her/him to call your back or I will ask them to do this for you when they come back in.'

- Always remember to be polite when screening any type of call whilst respecting the person's self-esteem. Even if it is the twentieth sales person you have had on that morning they have a legitimate job to do, but just make sure they are actually contacting the right person and redirect them if they are not.

- Be honest and say whether you are interested with sales-people or not. Don't simply ask them to put something in the post to get them off the telephone. Invariably they may take this as you being interested in their proposition and follow it up.

Don't feel guilty about screening your calls – it can be a very effective way of saving time.

Self-assessment

1. Log all telephone calls for a typical day. Note the number of incoming versus outgoing calls, and the percentage of people not available. Also log the average length of each call. Repeat this exercise every six to eight weeks.

2. Experiment with telephoning regular contacts at different times of the day. Are the calls shorter and more effective?

3. Make some time to read through your instruction manual for your telephone system – operate all the different functions confidently.

4. Ensure that your internal telephone directory is up-to-date.

5. Review your call log and ask:

   - Which calls took too long?
   - Which calls where low priority?
   - Were there any calls that could have been handled by someone else?
   - How were calls mis-routed?
   - How many times were you put on hold?
   - How many calls interrupted something more important?

Advanced telephone rapport

Matching

THE SKILL OF BUILDING CO-OPERATIVE RELATIONSHIPS

Rapport skills enable you to quickly put others at ease and create trust. Mastering the skill of building rapport requires awareness and flexibility on your part. The only two limits to your ability to produce results in gaining and creating rapport are the degree to which you can perceive other people's words, gestures and speech patterns and the way with which you can match them in the 'dance' of rapport.

The fundamental elements of matching on the telephone are:

VOICE

- Breathing rate
- Volume
- Tone
- Pitch
- Tempo
- Sounds
- Words.

OTHER ELEMENTS THAT YOU CAN MATCH

- Beliefs
- Values
- Interests
- Common experiences.

LEADING

Change the other person's behaviour by getting them to follow your lead eg leading them from complaining, into a more positive, optimistic frame.

This is one way to test that you do indeed have rapport. Having rapport, and hence being able to lead others, allows you to achieve mutually desired outcomes (eg reaching agreement!).

It also allows you to take responsibility for the outcome of all your interactions. It is, however, **a choice**. There may be some people with whom you might choose not have rapport. In which case you have the choice of mismatching.

Mismatching

Mismatching allows you to break rapport, to interrupt or to avoid communicating. To mismatch, simply alter your body and/or voice to make them different from the other person.

This will subtly and unconsciously interrupt the flow of communication giving you the opportunity to redirect the interaction. (NB if rapport is well established, you may find that the other person follows your behaviour as you mismatch, ie you are effectively leading them – you'll then have to keep changing your behaviour until they cease to follow you and you achieve a conclusive mismatch. For example, 'Hurrying' somebody off the telephone.)

General points about matching skills

NATURAL

The dance of rapport is what we do naturally. The barriers to rapport are often 'cultural' not behavioural.

EASY

It allows you to join the other person in their world or way of thinking and acting. Make it easy for others to communicate with you, practice rapport. Notice how you feel when you are matching different people.

PROACTIVE

It means actively and consciously developing your flexibility of thought and behaviour.

BE AWARE

Notice what happens when people get on well, they tend to match. Notice the opposite, when people are in disagreement, they mismatch. When you are not getting on well with someone, try matching.

SUSPEND JUDGEMENT

Experience the world as the other does – make them and their experiences/difficulties/joys much more understandable.

Avoid making decisions about the caller – it will cloud your concentration and judgement.

Liking the other person is not a prerequisite for rapport. What is, however, is mutual confidence in competence for the task in hand. If this cannot be established, consider changing the task.

Structuring a telephone call

Any telephone call should have four clear sections:

1. Opening and initiating control, agenda setting
2. Fact finding and questioning
3. Proposing ideas, solutions, options or information
4. Closing, confirming, summarising.

Figure 1: Telephone call structure

Open and initiate

1. BE PREPARED

Anticipate the needs of customers; have the information you need to hand; know and prepare for times of peak demand.

2. WELCOME

Greet customers and convey an attitude through tone of voice, verbal and body language, that you are interested and willing to help.

3. OUTGOING CALLS

Explain the purpose and benefit of the call and then check to ensure that the customer understands and agrees to proceed.

Gather information

4. LISTEN

Remembering the feelings and facts and the significant concerns that customers express.

5. ASK

Create effective questions to understand the customer's situation and what they really need to keep participating.

6. RESTATE

Let customers know you understand what was said – be sure to agree on what is being asked.

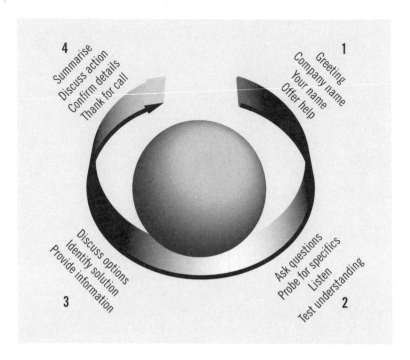

Figure 2: Key skills

Solutions and options

7. OFFER INFORMATION AND OPTIONS

Give customers useful information; provide them with choices. Use clear explanations and statements: 'package' information and options.

8. SET EXPECTATIONS

Let customers know what you can and cannot do; be clear; give specific details.

9. EXPLORE FURTHER NEEDS AND GET AGREEMENT

Ask questions; discuss features and benefits to help the customer visualise the usefulness of the service; assess the agreement level.

Confirm and close

10. ASK FOR A DECISION

Be direct, concise and confident in asking for commitment.

11. SUMMARISE AND CHECK

Summarise key points and check for satisfaction.

12. THANK

Express your appreciation to external and internal customers; make customers feel important.

13. FOLLOW UP

Ensure that what was promised to your customer is what they received; if passing your customer to another person in the organisation, make sure the transition is handled smoothly.

Difficult situations

14. HANDLE OBJECTIONS

Respond to objections stated by customers; change an objection into an opportunity.

15. HANDLE CHALLENGING SITUATIONS

Do your best to understand and help customers who may be angry or upset; recover from mistakes made by yourself or by your organisation; give bad news.

Telephone skills assessment

Using the scores below, complete the following questionnaire to assess your own telephone skills, or better still have someone complete it for you.

(1) to a very great extent – something you do extremely well

(2) to a great extent

(3) to a moderate extent

(4) to a small extent

(5) not at all – a real opportunity area!!

1. BEING READY

Anticipating the needs of customers; having the information I need or knowing where to get it, having all the equipment I need in working order; use of technology: knowing and preparing for times of peak demand.

(1) (2) (3) (4) (5)

2. WELCOMING

Greeting customers and conveying an attitude that shows them I am interested and willing to help through tone of voice, verbal language and body language.

(1) (2) (3) (4) (5)

3. MAKING THE CALL

Explaining the purpose and benefit of the call and then checking to ensure that the customer understands and agrees to proceed.

4. LISTENING

Hearing and remembering the feelings and facts and the significant concerns that my customers express.

5. ASKING

Creating effective questions to understand my customers' situation and what they really need to keep the customer participating.

6. RESTATING

Letting my customers know I understand what we said – both their feelings and facts of the situation; being sure that we agree on what they are asking.

7. OFFERING INFORMATION AND OPTIONS

Giving my customers useful information; providing them with choices. Using clear explanations and statements: 'packaging' information and options.

8. SETTING EXPECTATION AND GETTING AGREEMENT

Letting my customers know what I can and cannot do; being clear; giving specific details.

9. EXPLORING FURTHER NEEDS AND GETTING AGREEMENT

Asking good questions; discussing features and benefits to help the customer visualise the usefulness of the service; assessing the agreement level.

10. ASKING FOR A DECISION

Being direct, concise and confident in asking for commitment.

11. SUMMARISING AND CHECKING

Summarising key points and checking for satisfaction.

12. THANKING

Expressing appreciation to external and internal customers; making customers feel important.

13. FOLLOWING UP

Ensuring that what was promised to my customer is what they received; if passing my customer to another person in the organisation, making sure the transition is handled smoothly.

14. HANDLING OBJECTIONS

Responding to objections stated by my customers; changing an objection into an opportunity.

15. HANDLING CHALLENGING SITUATIONS

Doing my best to understand and help customers who may be angry or upset; recovering from mistakes made by myself or by my organisation; giving bad news.

NOTES

_____

_____

_____

THREE STRENGTHS

1. _____

2. _____

3. _____

THREE IMPROVEMENT AREAS

1. _____

2. _____

3. _____

Gathering information – key skills

The main skills needed in this stage are:

- listening and encouraging
- questioning
- confirming.

Listening and encouraging

It is vital that you hear and remember the feelings and facts and the significant concerns that customers express. This type of 'active' listening involves:

- small verbal acknowledgements, ah ah, yes, fine, I see, really
- taking notes and repeating back
- probing questions relating directly to the topic being discussed
- keeping quiet and letting the other person talk.

Silence is one of the most powerful techniques for getting information from others. Silence creates pressure on both parties. Good communicators learn to use silence at the appropriate time to draw the other person out and to avoid jumping in and answering their own questions.

KEY TIMES TO USE SILENCE ARE:

- just after the person has finished talking
- when you have asked an open question
- when you have closed for commitment
- whilst the person is talking.

When you have asked an open question always give the customer time to think and answer.

Questioning

Create effective questions to understand the customers' situation and what they really need. This keeps the customer participating and controls the call.

OPEN QUESTIONS

These questions invite the customer to give *more* than a yes/no answer. If used properly they stimulate information giving and avoid the interview becoming an interrogation. Open questions begin with the words:

- HOW?
- WHAT?
- WHY?
- WHEN?
- WHERE?
- WHO?

When you ask open questions you must allow the customer time to answer. Remember, the customer has to think in order to reply. Don't let the silence force you into letting them 'off the hook'.

Open questions should be used to gain information.

CLOSED QUESTIONS

These questions invite the customer to give a yes/no answer and because of this they should be avoided when you are looking for information specifically. This is because you have to ask a lot of questions to get the desired information.

Closed questions should be used to get **CONFIRMATION** when testing understanding or summarising.

Remember – ask closed questions for confirmation.

Avoid using them to gain information as they can **MISLEAD** or make you **ASSUME**.

Turning customer problems into opportunities

A customer who has had a problem solved well, is more loyal than one who has experienced no problem at all.

Most customers, when they telephone with a problem, focus only on the problem, complaining about what **DID NOT** happen, or **SHOULD HAVE** happened.

Focusing on what we don't want is much less effective. By trying to resist it we have to keep it in our mind. In order to avoid something, we have to know what it is we are trying to avoid.

How to turn problems into solutions

1. LABEL THE PROBLEM

Identify one vague generality in which a problem lurks and express it in words, even if they are vague and general.

ASK

What's the problem, specifically?

2. QUESTION AND CLARIFY

Second, apply clear questioning to a vague statement until it is reduced to a precise and clearly identified problem. Notice all the things you don't know about the vague generality, allow yourself to be curious and ask questions to recover the missing information.

ASK

'Who, what, when, where, how, and with whom, specifically?'

At this point you know who experiences what, when, where, how and with whom. This is only half a problem because a problem is defined as the difference between:

WHAT YOU'VE GOT	PROBLEM	WHAT YOU WANT
PRESENT STATE	SOLUTIONS	DESIRED STATE

3. IDENTIFY THE OPPORTUNITY

'What would you rather have?'

'What is the desired situation?'

'What would be better?'

4. CHECK 'POSSIBILITY' AND MANAGE EXPECTATIONS

ASK

'Is it possible...?'

'How would that be an improvement?'

'What needs to happen to make this possible?'

Handling customer questions

Customer questions usually imply interest and should therefore be seen as positive, for no one asks a question unless they are interested in some way with what is being discussed.

How we handle these questions is important, as they can increase our chances of furthering the call to a good result.

There are three ways in which a customer question can be handled:

1. By purely giving an answer to the customer question
2. By answering the customer question with a question
3. By answering the customer question with an answer and following it with a question.

Methods 1 and 2 do have their limitations.

METHOD 1
GIVING AN ANSWER TO THE CUSTOMER QUESTION

- Conversation could come to an end

- Customers might ask further questions

- Your answer might not be correct, or what the customer was expecting

- You could begin to give information because of the customer's interest

- You might give irrelevant information, leading to objection

- You could lose control.

METHOD 2
ANSWERING THE CUSTOMER QUESTION WITH A QUESTION

- You could be seen as smart

- It may look as though you're evading the question

- It doesn't give the customer an answer

- They could get annoyed.

METHOD 3
ANSWERING THE CUSTOMER WITH AN ANSWER AND FOLLOWING IT WITH A QUESTION IS RECOMMENDED

The reason being that firstly you give the customer an answer which they expect and secondly your follow-up question allows you not only to remain in control, but also helps the customer rationalise and expand upon the reason for their original question.

Structure for handling customer questions

- Answer the customer's question specifically whenever possible

- Ask a further question to either uncover a need area, or to close the conversation or issue, dependent upon where in the call the customer question arises.

EXAMPLE

Customer questions

'How much do your products cost?'

Answer

'We have a range of products to meet the various requirements of each of our customers, what is your specific application?'

or

'The price of this particular product is £   would you like to pay by credit card or use direct debit?'

We know that it will not always be easy to answer non-specifically, but by doing so, whenever possible, allows you to keep your options open and find out more about what the customer wants before you commit yourself.

Confirming – key skills

ASK FOR A DECISION

Be direct, concise and confident in asking for a commitment or agreement.

- *'Shall I go ahead and arrange that?'*
- *'Is that okay?'*

STATE AGREED ACTIONS

Be precise and definite in stating or agreeing steps and actions.

- *'The engineer will arrive between 12 noon and 3 pm, is that convenient for you?'*
- *'I will put the manual in the post tonight, so you should have it in the next day or two.'*

SUMMARISE AND CHECK

In summarising, the person repeats back information that has been agreed. As with testing understanding, it shows you have been listening and helps reduce misunderstanding.

Remember, summarising should be carried out throughout the call, not just at the review stage.

THANK

Express appreciation to external and internal customers; making customers feel important.

- *'Thank you for your call Mr/Ms _____*

FOLLOW UP

Ensuring that what was promised to your customer is what they received; pass the customer to another person in the organisation, make sure the transition is handled smoothly.

Difficult situations – key skills

The 'difficult' customers are the ones who really test our professionalism. It's easy to let customers who are angry and rude get under our skin and to take angry and rude remarks personally. But, we mustn't.

Remember, awkward customers are awkward to everyone; it's part of their lifestyle. We must be flexible when dealing with an awkward customer so that the 'win-win' situation is achieved each and every time.

HANDLE OBJECTIONS
Respond to customers' objections to your suggestions or requests; change an objection into an opportunity.

CHALLENGE SITUATIONS
This is doing your best to understand and help customers who may be angry or upset.

TALKATIVE CUSTOMER
Never
- show boredom or frustration
- interrupt and try to shout them down.

Always
- use their name
- listen for gaps in the conversation where it is possible to interject politely
- keep leading the conversation back to the point – again and again – by highlighting, confirming and summarising.

RUDE CUSTOMERS

People are ruder on the telephone, so don't take it personally.

Never

- get upset by the rudeness of an offensive customer

- be deliberately casual or icily superior to show an offensive customer what you think of them.

Always

- use their name

- stay cool, keep a professional distance and stay polite

- ignore their rudeness, remember that the offensive customer is offensive to everyone who serves them – not just you. Our job is not to turn them into a nice customer, simply to serve them with what they want.

The right way to interrupt a customer

1. Use their name clearly; 'Mr. SMITH...'

2. Apologise for the interruption; 'Sorry to interrupt you...'

3. State a reason for the interruption; 'In order to sort this out quickly, I need to know your account number...'

4. Ask a question to regain control, 'What is your account number please?'

Handling complaints

However hard we try to avoid them, mistakes will be made in every business. Therefore, what matters is how we handle the complaint arising from a mistake when it is brought to our attention.

As the caller cannot see what is happening or what effect his words are having, customers who make complaints over the telephone get more worked up and aggressive than they would face-to-face. We must take this into account when handling customer complaints by telephone.

Complaints are opportunities to put something that is wrong, right. Complaints should be viewed as another chance to give high customer care and satisfaction.

Remedy for complaints

Outlined below are general techniques for dealing with irate callers.

STAGE 1

- Listen carefully to what the caller has to say.

- Avoid the temptation to interrupt or give any explanation at this time. Allow the caller to state his views and feelings fully. He or she will not be prepared to listen to anything you have to say until he/she has done this.

- However, be sure to use encouraging phrases and sounds to reassure them of your interest.

STAGE 2

- Try to use neutral phrases to show that you understand the problem/emotion, eg 'I can see you are in a predicament', 'I can understand your feelings,' 'I appreciate your concern.' This will help them calm down and give you a basis for constructive dialogue.

- Apologise at this stage, only if appropriate. Avoid apologising repeatedly as it will only give the impression of grovelling.

STAGE 3

- Provided the caller has been allowed to state his or her views/feelings and care has been taken to avoid head-on arguments or disagreements, the caller should now have calmed down sufficiently to discuss the matter logically.

- Use straightforward language to explain solutions and discuss plans of action.

- If and when it is necessary to give bad news, try to counter it with something good.

- Ensure that any action required of you is done as speedily as possible.

Dealing with angry customers

Most customers are usually good-natured but occasionally you will talk to an angry customer. It is important that you have the skills and techniques to diffuse the customer's anger and get results from the call as well as reduce the bad feeling between the parties involved.

Techniques

When you have an angry customer on the telephone there are five techniques you can use to save the situation and get good results.

- Don't take anger personally.
- Allow the customer to talk.
- Acknowledge the customer's feelings.
- Find out what the specific problem is.
- Manage yourself.

Don't take anger personally, angry customers are not usually angry with you. You're merely a convenient target. Remember that the most important technique you can use in managing an angry customer is to manage yourself. It's important for you to control your temper and stay impartial. That way you'll accomplish two things. You will:

- avoid fuelling the anger, and
- keep control of the conversation.

Allow the customer to talk. Generally, an enraged customer will not stay angry for long. If there's no one to fight with, the customer will quieten down. So your first tactic is to remain quiet until the customer calms down.

DON'T MAKE EXCUSES

Control your natural urge to make excuses. You may know that the customer has made a mistake which is the cause of the problem, but they are not able to listen to your reasoning while they are angry. Your excuses will sound like attacks and will only serve to increase anger. So let the customer talk.

However, you are not obliged to listen to an abusive customer.

WHEN THE CUSTOMER BECOMES ABUSIVE

If a customer becomes so abusive that you can't let them continue to talk, you can:

- explain to them that you find it difficult to help while they are behaving in this manner
- tell them you'll call them back another time, or
- tell them they can speak to your manager, but only as a last resort.

RECOGNISE THE CUSTOMER'S FEELINGS

Acknowledge the customer's feelings. Many times you can calm the customer if you simply recognise their feelings. So, first allow them to talk, and then say something that lets them know that you recognise and acknowledge their anger.

EXAMPLE

'That must be very frustrating'

or

'That is a bad situation'

Do not use *'I understand how you feel'*

After that, you can begin to solve the problem.

Probe

Find out the specific problem. After you've helped the customer to calm down, probe to get all the information you can about the situation.

To retain a good relationship with the customer you need to solve the immediate problem or resolve the query.

Use your probing skills to find out about the problem. Use both open-ended and closed questions as the situation requires.

Benefits

Taking the time to probe for complete information benefits you in two ways. You are:

- able to solve the problem quicker and/or
- soothe the customer's anger.

By probing you may prevent the need for a return call to obtain the information you didn't get because you stopped probing too soon.

The attention and time you give the customer will probably soothe their anger. Most people can't stay angry for long if you're trying to be helpful. When your customer realises you're trying to help, they are usually co-operative with you.

Remember

All the customer really wants to know is what you are going to do about it and when. So:

- agree actions and
- follow-up.

Handling conflict

When one person 'attacks' another verbally it prompts a further attack or a defence response in the other person. These responses tend to spiral and get increasingly emotional, personal and further away from the specific issue because neither party find it easy to give way in this type of situation. These spirals are often started with minor 'irritants' such as 'I would expect you to know better', 'You always bring up that subject,' 'Here you go again', 'Why are you so stupid?' and in 80 per cent of occasions where this occurs people respond to an attack, with an attack.

HANDLING CONFLICT CAN BE VIEWED FROM TWO EXTREMES

Very vicious attack ——————————➤ **Supportive**

If you mess around in the middle, you can expect trouble.

Faced with an attack, people tend to hear nothing else, a very vicious attack will blot out the capacity of the listener to think about anything else because of the personal significance. Attacks therefore can be made unemotionally to a great effect if applied sparingly and unflinchingly. There must be no room for manoeuvre, do not give the listener a let-out by softening the blow, and don't try anything else with them until they have assimilated/recovered as they won't hear you.

At the other extreme, when faced with an attack, a combination of behaviour is required to handle the attack effectively so that the 'attacker' will become receptive to suggestions.

1. TEST UNDERSTANDING

This demonstrates that you are attentive and trying to take them seriously by concentrating on the specifics.

2. SEEK INFORMATION

As with *testing understanding* (above), this gives you the chance to get to the specific issues and start the behavioural change in the attacker. If you don't know the facts, you won't be able to propose a solution.

3. OPEN BEHAVIOUR

Taking the blame on yourself has nothing to do with the truth of the case, but has a way of taking the heat out of the confrontation. It makes it easier for them to climb down.

4. AGREEING

This shows you are on their side of the fence. They can hardly continue to attack you since they will then be effectively blaming themselves.

Using these behaviours in the above sequence will allow you to shape and change the behaviour of the attacker, from their attacking behaviour to a situation where they will be receptive of your suggestions and consequently build on them.

Assertiveness on the telephone

Assertive behaviour is the label given to a collection of behaviours that stem from the belief that our needs and wants are as important as those of the other person.

ASSERTIVE BEHAVIOUR IS WHEN YOU:

- stand up for your rights in a way that does not violate another person's rights.

SUBMISSIVE BEHAVIOUR IS WHEN YOU:

- fail to stand up for your rights or do so in such a way that others can easily disregard you

- express your thoughts, feelings and beliefs in an apologetic, cautious or self-affecting way

- fail to express your views and feelings altogether.

AGGRESSIVE BEHAVIOUR IS WHEN YOU:

- stand up for your rights in such a way that you violate the rights of another person

- express thoughts, feelings and beliefs in unsuitable and inappropriate ways, even though we may honestly believe these views to be right.

Why people behave aggressively or submissively

No one is likely to behave aggressively or submissively all the time. People tend to vary their behaviour. One occasion when people are more likely to react aggressively or submissively rather than assertively is in a conflict situation. This is all to do with the level of our self-esteem.

If our self-esteem is low, then we feel extremely anxious when a conflict arises. We feel insecure and threatened by the situation and the people in it. It is basic instinct when we feel threatened either to hit out (aggression) or to turn defensive (submission).

A further reason why aggressive and submissive behaviour occurs is that they do appear to have some advantages, eg aggressive behaviour is often successful in getting us what we want. It can give us a sense of power over others and helps us let off steam. Submissive behaviour can defuse a conflict very quickly by avoiding it. It helps us to escape the anxiety of confrontation. It also helps us to avoid feeling guilty about letting someone down or upsetting them.

As there are some advantages to aggressive and submissive behaviour, there is little incentive to change. However, there are many more benefits to assertive behaviour.

Recognising assertive, submissive and aggressive behaviour

PEOPLE WHO BEHAVE SUBMISSIVELY ARE LIKELY TO:

- make long rambling statements
- avoid making 'I' statements
- use qualifying phrases or words, eg 'Maybe...' 'Would you mind very much...' 'I wonder if I ...' 'Sorry to bother you but...'

- use filter words, eg 'Uh...' 'You know...'

- put themselves down, eg 'I seem to be hopeless at this...' 'I can't'

- use phrases that make it easier for others to ignore their needs or wants, eg 'It's not important really...' 'It doesn't matter.'

PEOPLE WHO BEHAVE AGGRESSIVELY ARE LIKELY TO:

- make excessive use of 'I' statements

- state their opinions as facts, eg 'That approach won't work...' 'That's rubbish'

- put others down, eg 'You must be joking...' 'That's only your opinion...' 'You cannot be serious'

- make a lot of use of the words: ought, must, should and have to

- be keen to attach blame to others, eg 'It was your fault...' 'Well I blame you.'

PEOPLE WHO BEHAVE ASSERTIVELY ARE LIKELY TO:

- make statements that are brief and to the point

- use 'I' statements, 'I think... I believe... I need'

- distinguish clearly between fact and opinion, eg 'In my experience...' 'My opinion is...' 'As I see it'

- avoid words like 'You should... you ought.'

- use open-ended questions to find out thoughts, opinions and wants of others, eg 'How does this affect you?...' 'What are your thoughts?'

- look for ways to resolve problems, eg 'How can we get round that...?' 'How about?'

THE ADVANTAGES OF ASSERTIVE BEHAVIOUR ARE:

- close working relationships
- greater confidence in yourself
- greater confidence in others
- increased self-responsibility
- savings in time and energy
- an increased chance of everyone winning.

Attitude

Your attitude is critical

Some people grab chances to satisfy and delight customers and others let them slip through their fingers. Some people can control their customer contact and they get the most out of it, while others seem to continually flounder. There's one reason for this self-doubt or lack of confidence – we don't believe in ourselves. We can be our own worst enemies by putting obstacles in the way of progress.

- It can't be done.
- It's too early.
- It's too late.
- It's impossible.

You must have positive belief in yourself. Don't try to achieve something – just *do* it.

Be positive: Some people look for the worst in situations, others look for the best. Make a point of looking for the positive aspects in any situation.

BELIEVE IN YOURSELF

From today, learn to like yourself more, take time out to feel good about yourself. Sell yourself to yourself. Talk positively to yourself.

- 'I can handle this.'
- 'I will succeed.'
- 'I am going to do this.'

Psychologists call this a 'positive mental attitude'. It can apply to your personal life as well as your working life.

DECIDE TO BE UNDERSTANDING

Believing in your success is the strongest factor between 'Winners' and 'Losers'. Many people are stuck on the 'if only' attitude.

- If only I was younger/older.
- If only I was thinner/prettier/more handsome.
- If only I was more clever.

We are all born with a winning chance but along the way we experience disappointments which are recorded in our brain, inhibiting our ability for success.

Belief is the driving force behind all achievements.

DON'T BE A QUITTER

Making mistakes is inevitable. The person who says that they never made a mistake, has never done anything. Accept that you will make mistakes – but stick at it until you get it right.

The more you talk and act like a winner, the more of a winner you'll be!

An action plan for self-development

- Work together as a team.
- Strive to improve your performance.
- Seek out opportunities.
- Experiment/try different things.
- Be positive.
- Talk about your success.
- Set yourself goals and objectives.
- Review your experiences.
- Tolerate short-term discomforts.
- Be determined to win!
- Be ready to do whatever it takes.

Telephone skills – best practise summary

HELPFUL HINTS – THE DO'S

- Be prepared – have pen and paper handy at all times.
- Answer promptly, clearly and with a smile. Introduce yourself in a professional manner.
- Establish and then use the caller's name early in the telephone conversation.
- Ask open-ended questions to establish the facts and exact requirements.
- When listening, make 'listening voices' such as 'yes,' 'really' etc.

- Make notes and confirm back key points so that the caller knows that you are being attentive.

- Use assertive behaviour to control the call.

- Give the customer a choice of actions wherever possible.

- Take proper messages on message pads noting date and time.

- Smile.

- Complete the call with a commitment to action.

- Let the caller put the telephone down first.

HELPFUL HINTS – THE DON'TS

- Don't leave the telephone unattended for any length of time.

- Avoid the use of company jargon.

- Beware of smoking, eating and drinking on the telephone, people can hear it and it sounds unprofessional.

- Don't interrupt! Wait for a natural pause or for the customer to take a breath, then interject politely using their name.

- Don't bluff or waffle. If you don't know the answer – say so, and undertake to find out.

- Beware of speaking too quickly, too slowly or too monotonously.

- Don't assume anything.

- Don't leave the customer hanging on without an explanation of what is happening.

Customer service – application assignments

The following exercises will help you to transfer the skills and methods from this section into your work.

1. Make a checklist of at least ten things that you would listen for in an effective telephone call as a customer – including whatever is important to you. Make sure each item is specific and measurable. For example, instead of 'answering the telephone quickly', try 'answers within 3-4 rings.'

2. Using a local or national newspaper or magazine, telephone five companies to enquire about their products or services. Mark each one using your checklist. Make a note of anything else you notice and decide the best and worst call.

3. Repeat the exercise above for a few companies or organisations where you are an existing customer – perhaps invent some questions or complaints. For example, query an entry on your bank statement, ask for a copy bill from a utility company, etc.

4. When an organisation gives you cause to complain – pick up the telephone and do it! Make a note of your call, use a checklist, and see how well or poorly they handle your call.

5. Telephone five companies with whom your business competes.

6. Record two or three calls every day, perhaps at random. Play back and listen for ways that you can improve.

7. Have a friend or colleague telephone your office and leave a message for you when you are not in. How well was the call handled? When and how accurate was your message?

GAINING APPOINTMENTS
BY TELEPHONE

The importance of proactive prospecting	70
Sales is a numbers game	72
The most important step in the sales process	77
Ten top tips on making appointments	79
Making appointments: planning and preparation	83
Getting past gatekeepers	91
How to structure a call	97
Cold-calling blues	104
'Warm-calling': A three-step method to increase your sales	108
Ideal appointment times	118
Example call	119
Prospect tracking	121
Appointments – application assignments	124

The importance of proactive prospecting

The importance of prospecting by telephone in developing new sales opportunities cannot really be overstated. It is the one element of the sales cycle upon which all other activities depend.

Without a regular supply of well-qualified and active prospects, there is no opportunity to demonstrate your superior knowledge, selling skills or company services and products.

If there is one thing that a sales person – any sales person – can do in the short-term to increase their sales results, it is to increase the number of active prospects, and that means increasing the number of appointments, and that usually means picking up the telephone.

Attracting customers by the telephone is one of the most effective methods of prospecting; consider the alternatives for a moment:

1. PERSONAL CALLING

Personal cold-calling, that is knocking on either business or personal doors, is one of the hardest, and perhaps the least practised sales skill today. Modern technology has meant that we no longer have to walk the pavements in search of new prospects.

However, this does not mean to say that it is not effective. Indeed, in certain situations it can be extremely effective. For instance, if you are calling on one particular organisation on a trading estate or high street, a quick call to the buildings either side can very often result in a new contact, and it has not cost anything other than a few minutes.

The issue of cold-calling in the sales process is covered in greater detail on page xx.

2. DIRECT MAIL

Direct mail is, on most occasions, an extremely high volume activity. Where it is used to generate appointments, these leads and enquiries nearly always have to be followed up by telephone, so the telephone appointment making skills are still relevant. The purpose of direct mail is to attract new leads and perhaps make several new sales.

Direct mail serves to:

a. introduce the company

b. warm the customer ready for your call

c. prompt the customer to respond to the mailer.

However, the response rate of direct mail can be dramatically increased when it is combined with proactive telephone approaching, so once again the skills of making appointments and following up leads by telephone are very important.

Consider for a moment how many potential customers you can contact and speak to in a two-way conversation (mail is always a one-way paper based communication) during a working day? 30, 40, 50, 100? These potential prospects could be spread across the country or even the world.

The telephone is quick, convenient, cost-effective and instant. When compared with face-to-face cold-calling there is almost no comparison. A telephone marketer can contact more people in an hour than somebody in a car could cover in a day.

Increasingly more and more companies especially professional service firms and consultants are realising the power and potential of using the telephone to generate business and in particular appointments. Sales time is precious, and new leads and new customers are hard to come by. *Mastering the skills of getting appointments by telephone, can ensure that you are in control of your sales results.*

Sales is a numbers game

Many years ago Rank Xerox, along with other large and very significant office equipment companies, developed an approach to selling which set the tone for a generation.

The slogan of *calls equals demonstrations equals sales* was spread around the world in countless sales training courses and repeated endlessly in thousands of sales meetings.

The basic idea is that the number of sales that you are able to generate is directly proportional to the number of proposals or demonstrations or quotations that you do, which in turn is directly in proportion to the number of appointments that you make.

It therefore follows that the number of telephone calls you make is also related directly to the number of appointments you are able to generate.

'90% of success is showing up'

Woody Allen

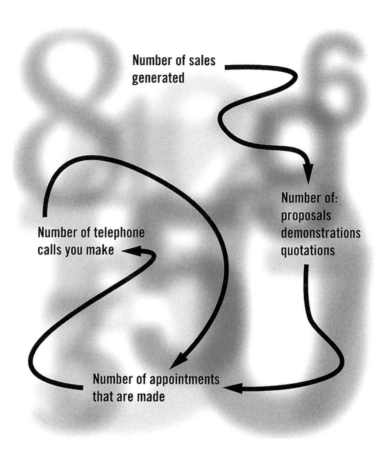

Figure 3: Calls and sales are proportional

If we imagine for a moment that somewhere out there are ten potential prospects and customers waiting for you to call them. However, you don't know who they are, you don't know which companies they are or whereabouts they are located.

The only thing that you may have is a list or a card index box and directory containing perhaps hundreds of names. You simply have to find them.

They might be the first ten calls that you make, whilst statistically unlikely, nonetheless within the realms of possibility. They might be the last ten calls that you make.

However, unless you make the calls you will never know. Indeed, unless you make the calls you will never find them. Now you may be able to increase over time your skills and technique on the telephone, and very often a small change or improvement can lead to dramatically different results. One of the most fundamental principles is that you have to make enough telephone calls.

Filling the funnel

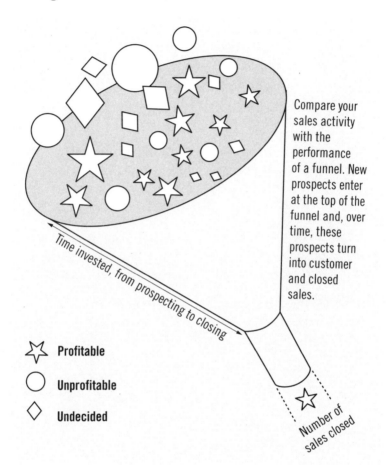

Compare your sales activity with the performance of a funnel. New prospects enter at the top of the funnel and, over time, these prospects turn into customer and closed sales.

Time invested, from prospecting to closing

☆ Profitable

○ Unprofitable

◇ Undecided

Number of sales closed

Figure 4: Gaining appointments using the funnel method

Think of the sales pipeline as a large funnel. In the top put a large quantity of suspects and prospects. As they pass through the funnel some of these, through a process of qualification and also presentation, are sifted out and the best few are left. You can then go on to try and close and convert these into orders. Only a percentage of these, however, actually become orders.

Give people a reason to agree to an appointment.

Gaining appointments by telephone is a 'filling the funnel activity'. It is the part of the sales process where we put new suspects, leads and prospects into the top of the funnel before they are worked on.

Whilst there are things we can do to move prospects through the funnel quicker, either by better presentation skills, offering special discounts, better closing, quicker follow up and so on, the inputting of new prospects into the funnel really does take solid activity.

There are very few short cuts and it is one of the most basic principles of becoming a successful sales person that you have to master the skills and techniques of filling the funnel proactively using the telephone.

The most important step in the sales process

There are some eight or nine steps or sequences in a typical sales cycle. Prospecting, qualifying, identifying needs, presenting, handling objections, closing the sale, follow-up, and gaining referrals and repeat business are just some of these. However, without the first, none of the others are possible. The paradox is that telephoning for appointments, often referred to as cold-calling, is one of the most disliked, neglected and least enjoyable parts of the sale process.

Many sales professionals only seem to do it when they have to, and their sales suffer an up and down roller-coaster ride as a result. However, gaining appointments by telephone can be a lot of fun and be extremely rewarding. It is possible to look back over a series of daily activity records and see continual and definite improvement of both generating appointments and conversion into sales.

Influencing tomorrow's sales today

> **INFLUENCING TOMORROW'S SALES TODAY**
>
> By being organised and prepared every day it is possible to make a head start on tomorrow's sales today.
>
> - Make the most of your telephone
> - Look through your contact cards or database for possible calls to be made tomorrow
> - Contact potential customers early

Whilst it is impossible to manage results, it is more than possible to manage activity. By spending time every day in working the telephone, sifting through your cards, contacting potential prospects, making appointments by telephone you are systematically and methodically building tomorrow's future business.

Just in the same way as an athlete can prepare for a competition by training regularly basis, so you can prepare for great sales results by picking up the telephone every day and contacting ten or more people who have the potential to buy from you.

The number of appointments that you need to make will, of course, be based on and influenced by the type of products and services that you sell, how new you are to your particular position or territory, and the turnover and the potential for repeat business from your customers. There are few businesses, however, that could not benefit from having more or better customers and that means proactive prospecting using the telephone.

> **Keep a list, notebook or file of 'target prospects' and spend time everyday on prospecting, working through one-by-one.**

Ten top tips on making appointments

*Your organisation might well have a strong advantage in the market, and a very compelling story, however **you** must make the first approach.*

Here are some vital principles that can make the difference between success and failure when gaining appointments by the telephone with target prospects, customers or clients.

Any one of these on their own can make a difference to your results in converting cold calls into new clients. When combined together, they become a powerful sales approach.

1. ONLY SELL THE APPOINTMENT.

When talking to a potential prospect on the telephone, it is very easy to become distracted and begin talking about products, services, etc. However, this is a great mistake. Selling actual goods and services over the telephone is a real skill and is a very different approach to selling an appointment (this is covered in the next part).

2. MAKE APPOINTMENTS IN ADVANCE

This will create the impression that you are organised, professional and busy (!) and you are more likely to find space in the prospects' diary.

3. YOU CAN'T ANSWER OBJECTIONS

When a prospect gives you an objection, such as they are too busy, they don't have the time, they already have an existing supplier or provider and so on, these are very difficult to isolate and outweigh on the telephone.

Even if we could, the prospect would probably not allow us the time to do this. Instead, we simply have to acknowledge them and emphasise our reasons for meeting.

4. DON'T PUT THINGS IN THE POST

The two reasons why people put things in the post to prospects, is because it is easy and it is low rejection. It is an easy way for prospects to get you off the telephone.

The only reason you should put anything in the post is to prove that you keep your word and also to confirm your appointment and/or build on an agreement.

Consider for a moment if you stopped putting things in the mail, if you had no brochures, leaflets or letters to send out, would the number of appointments that you are currently getting increase or decrease?

5. FOLLOW UP EVERY LEAD

Every sales opportunity, every prospect, every telephone number and contact is a vital one.

We need to manage every prospect as if they were the most important one. So, if you have a bottom drawer full of old leads taken from an exhibition or half used mailing lists, or card index systems that you haven't touched for months, then make it your priority to get them sorted out and followed up.

6. STAY IN TOUCH

One of the simplest things that you can do to increase your success rate in gaining new prospects (and developing business) is to call each one every three to four months. By building a systematic 90 day cycle into your prospecting, you can, over time, build a substantial contact base and a regular stream of new business leads.

> When someone says 'no' to your request for an appointment, it may be 'not now... not this month'. Simply leave it a few weeks and try again.

Consider how much easier it is, both psychologically and also in terms of managing the conversation, to speak to somebody you have spoken to before, no matter how briefly. Not only do you have a reference to talk about when you speak to them, but also the level of resistance may be much lower. For instance, consider how much easier it is to get past the receptionist when we know the company and we want to speak to the individual.

Remember that when we get a 'no' on the telephone, it simply means 'not now', 'not today', 'not this month'. If you are targeting your market correctly, the prospect will buy at some time from somebody. If you don't contact them then somebody else will.

7. MAKE 25 TO 50 CALLS EVERY DAY OR WEEK

The actual activity level that you choose will obviously depend on how many appointments you need and your type of business. However, one of the most effective habits of a successful and professional sales person is that they schedule time, usually every day, for prospecting. Make sure you develop a habit and a routine for spending at least one hour every day in an intensive telephoning campaign. Call it your golden hour and have one intensive hour of solid telephone calling.

In that one hour, telephoning should be all that you do, make as many as 30 telephone calls. This will, over time, generate several appointments a day. Do not use 'lack of time' as an excuse – **MAKE** time.

8. KEEP GOOD RECORDS

Information on prospects and what you have discussed with them does not need to be in depth. A few key words to jog your memory is usually all that is required. It is also important to make a note of when you have called people and they have not been available, this will allow you to judge the time to call them back and whether or not it is appropriate.

9. GET A TRACKING SYSTEM THAT WORKS FOR YOU

One of the things that increases call reluctance, or the fear and reluctance and resistance to making telephone cold calls, is a lack of organisation. By not having clear lists of people to telephone, by not having enough people to telephone, we actually encourage ourselves to procrastinate and put off making those calls.

By not having an accurate computer database, or tracking 'system' that allows us to track call backs and monitor information, we can also give ourselves excuses as to why we shouldn't make calls. The importance of a tracking system is twofold, one is to make sure that we do follow-up every lead, and two is that we give ourselves no excuses not to make the calls.

10. BE PERSISTENT

Persistence works when nothing else does. When prospecting by telephone you will need to be persistent, professional and patient. There are no quick fixes, there are no easy answers, there are simply more effective ways and less effective ways, and both take a good degree of persistence. However, be reassured that persistence does work.

By simply making the right number of calls on a persistent basis, regardless of your current skill level you will be successful in making appointments. The statistics work *for* you as well as *against* you. If you telephone 100 people, you may only find 50 of them in, and of those 50 you may only get to speak to 25 or 30, and of those 25 you may only get two or three appointments. At least you have got two or three more appointments than you would have got if you hadn't made the 100 calls. The two or three appointments might be in the first ten calls that you make or the last ten calls that you make. You will never know until you make them.

Making appointments: planning and preparation

When making appointments by telephone it is the planning and preparation that can often secure and ensure success.

Before you pick up the telephone there are several things that you need to consider which make the call easier and much more effective. You also need to be able to sustain your telephoning activity. It is not enough to simply spend a day on the telephone every now and then when your appointment levels begin to dip, instead a regular consistent approach to generating prospects and appointments is required.

This means thinking through *who* you are going to call, *what* you are going to say, *how* you are going to try to persuade to see you, *how* to ask for the appointment and *how* to follow-up and progress that suspect into a prospect.

Opening the call

Opening the call is one of the most vital stages of any telephone call. The old adage that you never get a second chance to make a good first impression is as true for telephoning as it is for face-to-face meetings. The first 15 to 16 seconds of any telephone call will establish your credibility and level of confidence. You may be able to rescue a bad start but it is much better to start off well.

'Make friends in low places'. It will be progressively harder to gain appointments the more senior you target contacts.

Building interest and qualifying

One of the things that we need to think about is *who* we want to see. In the first instance we might want to visit anybody that will see us, this will depend on what we are selling and to whom. We may, however, begin to become more selective, and we can afford to if we get better at making appointments by telephone. Then we will not just have to see anybody who grants us an appointment, we can actually choose where we go and spend our time. We can highlight the accounts and the customers who provide the greatest opportunity, and perhaps the greatest buying urgency.

As time is short on the telephone we have to build interest and qualify the customer very quickly, often in a matter of seconds and minutes. We may also need to trust our intuitions about the particular customer more than we would if we were meeting face-to-face. We may also have to recognise that the customers themselves will be using their intuition more than they would normally do.

Overcoming objections

This may come as a surprise but nobody is actually sitting waiting for you to call to offer your products or services. There are, however, people out there who are looking for what you are selling or have to offer right now. Your mission or purpose in telephoning is to try and find these people. One thing potential customers will have in common is that when you ask them if you can come and see them, the chances are you will get some reasons why not. They might be too busy, they may already have existing suppliers they are reasonably happy with, they may not see any point at meeting up at the moment. You need to be able to overcome these objections and gain the appointment.

This is one of the primary skills and the thing that so many sales-people find difficult.

Closing a telephone call and asking for an appointment is very much the same as closing a sale and asking for an order. You are asking the customer, or in this case a prospect for agreement.

You are making a proposal, which should hold benefits and features for the prospect, just like in asking for the order – if you don't ask, you don't get!

Handling objections

EXAMPLES:

'TELL ME ABOUT IT NOW'

I wish I could, but it does depend on your exact requirements. I would be able to give you more information on how our service works and why it's different when we meet. Would next Thursday at 9.30 am or 3.45 pm be suitable?

'I'M TOO BUSY'

I do appreciate that, and that's why I'll call in advance. All I would need is about 20 minutes to introduce myself and explain the flexibility and competitiveness of our approach. How does Tuesday morning look? Or perhaps Wednesday afternoon at 4.00 pm?

'I DON'T DEAL WITH THIS'

Oh? I'm sorry, who does deal with this? I see, it might be best to meet with yourself first, as the person who is responsible for introducing new ideas, new projects. Shall we say Wednesday at 12.00 or perhaps at 4.15 pm?

'SEND ME A BROCHURE'

I would be only too pleased to send you our brochure, but it is very general and quite brief. I would really like to introduce myself and show you some important information that I can't post – ways to develop new clients and increase revenue/profit from existing renewals. How does this Friday look at 2.30 pm or perhaps next Monday at 10.30 am?

State as a purpose for a meeting that you would like to 'Introduce yourself or meet in *person*'. This will make it harder for the customer to put you off.

'YOU'RE WASTING YOUR TIME'

Well, if nothing else, it will ensure that you keep up-to-date and are getting the best service from your existing provider, I promise to be brief... Perhaps next Tuesday at 11.00 am would suit you or Wednesday afternoon at 2.30 pm?

'I AM NOT INTERESTED'

Can I ask what makes you say that? (This will lead to other objections, see below.)

'WE USE ANO CREDIT SUPPLIER'

I appreciate this, Mr Prospect, and this is the reason I am ringing you. We have a really flexible approach, and are very competitive. We would like to think that we can supplement, not replace, your existing provider. Now would Thursday at 10.00 am or Friday at 9.00 am be the more convenient time to you?

'ANO DO A REALLY GOOD JOB FOR US'

I realise that, and that is why I wanted to contact you. We have a really flexible approach, and are very competitive. We would like to think that we can supplement, not replace, your existing provider... is Monday afternoon suitable or Tuesday at 10.00 am?

'I'VE HEARD THAT YOUR RATES ARE TOO EXPENSIVE'

You may be right, but I don't think that I can make any relative cost quotation at the moment because it depends on your particular requirements. Perhaps you will give me a few minutes of your time next week when we can discuss this in more depth. Would Tuesday at 10.00 am be suitable or Friday at 4.00 pm?

Closing the call

Once you have gained commitment you need to get off the telephone as fast and politely as possible. This means swiftly and efficiently confirming the details, asking any final questions, thanking the customer for their time and moving on.

Doing this efficiently can lead to a level of positive expectancy when you meet the customer, doing it poorly may result in the appointment being cancelled.

Setting objectives

It is said the starting point of achieving anything is knowing what it is that you want to achieve. Before you pick up the telephone or before you begin your telephoning prospecting hour, *take time to define your objectives* for each call.

One of the ways that we can also deal with failure and rejection when we don't get an appointment on the telephone, is to think of it slightly differently by setting ourselves realistic objectives. Consider for a moment these three types of objective.

Ideal objective

Obviously if you are telephoning to gain an appointment, your ideal objective is to get an appointment. Whilst this is our total focus for the telephone call, and should remain a clear goal at all times, we also know that not every call will achieve an ideal objective. This does not mean that we should easily settle for a second best, instead we should also recognise that there are other objectives that we can achieve which can allow us to feel that the call has been a success.

Secondary objective

A secondary objective, is the next best thing that we could achieve from a telephone call. It is an objective that is perhaps more realistic, and allows us to have a sense of satisfaction and achievement on completion of the telephone call. For example, if we were on a telephone call and realised after one or two closing questions that we weren't going to be able to get an appointment with this prospect, our secondary objective would then be to find a time in the future when we could agree to call them back to check their needs at that time.

So, if this is our objective and we agree this with the prospect on the telephone we can then end the call on a note of achievement. We then need to make sure that we have a tracking system that will allow us not to forget to do this, or otherwise the objective is worthless.

SAMPLE OBJECTIVES
1. Make a good impression
2. Gain information and leave the door open for future contact
3. Gain an appointment

A FALL BACK OBJECTIVE

Even if we fail to get our appointment, and the prospect reassures us that they have no future need for our services, then we can at least say that we have achieved a fall back objective of eliminating a prospect from our list. This in itself can be a sense of achievement. By eliminating and sifting through our prospect base, we are getting closer to finding the nuggets of gold that exist.

Attitude and motivation

One of the most important things, indeed perhaps the most important thing, when telephoning for appointments is your attitude and the level of motivation. It has been said that an engaged tone is a sign that you are just not thinking positively enough! Whilst this is difficult to prove, and perhaps even more difficult to believe, there is clearly no doubt that your positive attitude, and level of motivation has a direct influence on how many telephone calls you can make and also how successful those calls will be.

For example, can you imagine how positive your attitude would be and how motivated you would be to make telephone calls if you knew that every telephone call you made would work out well.

You need to have that positive attitude every time you pick up the telephone to dial.

Every call counts

If it takes 100 telephone calls to get five or ten appointments it doesn't matter. You would make the telephone calls and try and improve either your targeting or your conversational skills.

> Every time you get a 'No', is a sign that you are one call closer to getting a 'YES'.

The fact is that without making those 100 calls you would not have found those five or ten appointments.

In this respect *every call counts*, this is the attitude that will ensure that you stay motivated and keep motivated to make those calls. We are never quite sure what the next call will hold for us, just in the same way we are never quite sure exactly what to expect in each appointment, what we may think might be a small or insignificant customer, may turn out to completely surprise us and may go on to lead us to a lot more business.

Failure is the essence of success

In this respect one of the fundamental principles of professional selling is very true for gaining appointments by the telephone. The only real measure of success is how much you are failing. The more '**NOs**' you are getting relatively speaking, the more likely you are going to get an increasing number of people saying '**YES.**'

In selling, and in particular in gaining appointments by the telephone, the only two types of failure are not making enough calls in the first place and giving up on each call too soon.

Getting past gatekeepers

The term 'gatekeeper' is a polite and respectful definition of anybody whose job it is to direct or screen calls around an organisation. These might be receptionists, secretaries, administration assistants or personal assistants.

To many salespeople these gatekeepers are the most frustrating and the most difficult parts of gaining appointments by telephone. They seem to be at odds with everything the sales person is trying to achieve. It is also not uncommon for salespeople to become slightly paranoid about certain individuals in certain organisations, believing they have something against them personally. Nothing could be further from the truth. Gatekeepers have a very important and essential job to do in any organisation, your role as a sales person is to help them achieve that job and also to achieve yours. Outlined below are some key points to consider when trying to get past secretaries and receptionists.

Your voice tone should be both friendly and confident, not too forceful or 'pushy'.

Indirect questioning

By using a slightly more amenable form of questioning, being slightly more indirect, we can actually increase our chances of getting through to our decision-maker. For example, instead of asking 'Could I speak to Mr Johnson?' try asking 'Could you tell me if Mr Johnson is in today?', or 'Is Mr Johnson the right person to talk to regarding exhibitions?'. The receptionist or secretary will hear your question and very often put you through.

Treating with respect

It is vital that you treat every receptionist, secretary or assistant that you meet with the utmost respect, friendliness, helpfulness and sense of importance. There is absolutely nothing to be gained by being rude, assertive or in any way speaking down to gatekeepers. Their whole job is geared around helping people. You need to get them on your side.

One of the simplest ways is to simply ask 'I wonder if you can help me?'. This wonderful expression, when used sincerely and with a friendly tone of voice, is almost irresistible. After all, they are in the business of helping their managers do their job.

We need to relate what we are doing to help their manager do their job better. Get them on your side by understanding their role and helping them to help you. State clearly who you are and why you are calling, and do not under any circumstances try any clever techniques to disguise why you are calling or who you are calling from. In the end this will be self-defeating.

Using the backdoor

If you are trying to contact senior managers, or people higher up an organisation, you will find them increasingly harder to get to the further up you go. This is not just simply because they have better or more rigid gatekeepers, it is also perhaps because they are generally less able to talk to you or less willing to talk to you. Sometimes it can be much more useful to take time to use the backdoor approach.

Always try and get direct line extensions from receptionists or assistants.

This normally means making contacts lower down the organisation, perhaps on a more operational basis gaining a foothold, gaining information and rapport and then using these contacts to take you steadily up the organisation and through to other people.

Persistent without being a pest

When telephoning to make an appointment the chances are very high that you won't actually be able to speak to the person that you are telephoning. There are, therefore, a few simple rules that you need to adopt in terms of leaving messages and being on hold.

Only go on hold once, and then for only 30 seconds. To go on hold any longer will be self-defeating. You could actually be getting on with another call and also our attitude and motivation is diminishing by the second. So simply agree to go on hold for a short while (20 to 30 seconds) and then if the secretary comes back to ask you to call back, find out at what time might be convenient.

Never ask people to call you back. Not only will only one in a hundred actually bother to do so, but when they do, you may well be on the telephone, or probably can't remember their details.

Do not leave a message. Unless it is a prospect that you have spoken to before that knows you, do not leave any message as to who you are, the fact that you have called, or why you are calling. This can alert the person that you are trying to speak to them and they may then leave specific instructions on how you should be dealt with!

Do not call the same company more than three times in a day. More than this is definitely being a pest. Unless they are particularly keen to talk to you, always follow this rule and you will never be accused of being pushy or pestering.

POSITIVE PROOF THAT PERSISTENCE PAYS

- The key to successful prospecting and building a solid and steady stream of prospects, customers and sales is undoubtedly the quality of persistence. The ability to keep on trying, to make one more call, to try one more close for that appointment, to be delayed without being deterred, is a rare and valuable commodity.

- It is a skill that has absolutely no value to the person who has no goals... they will have nothing to persist towards.

- If everything else remains equal between two rival salespeople; if they have the same skills and quality of approach, the same product and prices, the difference may only be the persistence of one person over the other.

- As a sales manager once explained to me when I was a young and struggling salesman 'You only start selling when the customer says **NO**!' You don't actually start to earn your money or use your craft until you get those NOs, and begin to use persistence to find a way round them. This is the key to understanding persistence – you don't have to have it, you just have to **USE** it.

- Many research surveys demonstrate the importance of this persistence factor. The first followed the fortunes of several thousand salespeople and studied how many contacts they had with each customer before they closed the sale. They found that:

  - *80 per cent of sales were made after the fifth contact*
  - *48 per cent of salespeople gave up after the first contact and won just two per cent of the sales*
  - *73 per cent of salespeople gave up after the second contact and won three per cent of the sales*
  - *85 per cent of salespeople lasted until the third contact and won five per cent of the sales*
  - *90 per cent of salespeople wouldn't try after the fourth contact, when ten per cent of the sales were made*
  - *Only ten per cent of salespeople continue past the fourth contact, and end with 80 per cent of the business.*

- The second survey studied control groups of 100 cold-call prospects. From this study they concluded the following:

  - *Ten say 'Yes' and agree to see/visit you*
  - *Ten say 'No', and are completely not interested*
  - *20 ask you to call back*
  - *50 are not available, and*
  - *Ten want more information.*

- If you want to get a bigger slice of the 100 prospects, the only real way is to use persistence to recall the 50 who are 'not available' and carefully and systematically progress and track the 30 who want more information or ask to be called back. This, and this alone, can double or triple your sales productivity, with everything else remaining constant.

Handling assistants – notes

Assistants are important, especially directors' assistants. Be polite. Remember they are there to protect their boss from salespeople.

- Use them if you can to make the appointment or to gain additional information.

- If after all your efforts they will not let you through to the M.A.N. (Money Authority Need) try the following:

  - Write to them.

  - Telephone before 9.00 am or after 5.30 pm.

  - Try to arrange an appointment through them.

- Make the secretary work hard for information. If she has to keep coming back to you for information she may feel embarrassed and put you through. For example, use M.A.N.'s name (this implies you know them) and ask to be put through.

- When she asks you who is calling, give your name, followed by *'Can you put me through, please.'*

- When she asks you what company, say – *'XYZ, can you put me through please.'*

- If she asks what it is about have a response ready which is reasonably technical eg *'Yes, I want to ask him some questions about your recent merger, can you put me through please.'*

How to structure a call

Introduction

As with prospecting in general, effective sales-people follow a process to help focus their time and efforts. The telephone prospecting call outline has three components:

- opening
- progressing
- concluding.

> If you are telephoning to get an appointment – state the reason clearly at the beginning of the call. Honesty is more persuasive.

OPENING

An effective opening includes the following:

STEP	ACTIONS
Connecting	Confirm the prospect's name and introduce yourself and your company. Refer to common acquaintances, associations and so on.
Purpose	State your reason for contacting the prospect.
Benefit	State the benefit to the prospect of talking with you.
Check	Check for interest and agreement. If appropriate, ask if it is a convenient time to talk.

> Using the words 'new', 'interesting' or 'different' can create compelling curiosity to find out more.

PROGRESSING

Progressing includes the following:

STEP	ACTIONS
Ask questions.	Ask questions about the area of your business.
Use a capability statement (when needed).	Link the company's capabilities to the customer's probable needs. Answer 'Why xyz company?'
State the benefits and reason for an appointment.	Introduce yourself. Discuss some new, interesting or different changes/ideas.
Handle objections.	Use the handling objections process if the potential client raises objections.

CONCLUDING

Concluding includes the following:

STEP	ACTIONS
Summarise and check.	Confirm the appointment and set a time and place (if not done).
Recommend and check.	Thank the prospect and express enthusiasm about the meeting.

Making progress

When progressing with an appointment-making call, you should demonstrate to the customer that XYZ Ltd may be able to help solve business problems. The capability statement should:

- be tailored to the specific industry, and
- include the pertinent benefits XYZ Ltd can offer that customer.

The capability statement should be delivered after the customer has agreed to the purpose of the call.

Example:

- Open the call stating the purpose – to explore ways in which XYZ Ltd might help the customer's business meet its goals.

- State the benefit – investing time in the call might provide some new information about products and services that the customer could find useful.

- Check – to gain agreement to the purpose.

'Name dropping' or referring to similar clients/ applications can be a good door-opener and gains credibility.

Progress the call:

- Qualify the prospect.

- Deliver a capability statement, if needed, by describing ways in which XYZ Ltd has helped businesses such as the customer's solve similar problems.

KEEPING IT SIMPLE

Keep your conversation with the prospect on a more general and conceptual level. Do not get drawn into nitty-gritty details or you may find yourself in deeper than you want to be. If you find a customer who wants to hear your pitch, try to 'defuse and defer.' Remember that your purpose in making the initial call is to get an appointment, **not** to tell the prospect everything that XYZ has to offer.

Effective capability statements – examples

Below are the criteria for effective capability statements, followed by segments of sample statements that are either more or less effective at meeting the criteria.

CRITERION	LESS EFFECTIVE	MORE EFFECTIVE
Setting the stage for a common understanding.	XYZ Ltd has been in business for over ten years. Years ago we started developing value-added services for our customers. Many of our customers participate in these programmes.	XYZ Ltd has been in business for over ten years. We have developed several programmes to increase service and meet the needs of companies like yours.

CRITERION	LESS EFFECTIVE	MORE EFFECTIVE
Linking XYZ Ltd corporate capabilities to the customer's probable needs.	XYZ Ltd is the only company that can guarantee a reduced cost on your mobile telephone calls.	We can help you, for example, to choose the right tariff level, if you are interested in reducing call costs.
Being specific enough to be interesting.	Many establishments are trying to save money. XYZ Ltd has helped many companies do this quickly.	Companies like yours are often trying to reduce their call costs. XYZ Ltd has helped businesses like yours save over 20% during a 12 month period.
Being broad enough not to close off options.	XYZ Ltd helps establishments increase service quality.	Our product will give you improved network access and support.

Developing your own capability statements

The purpose of this exercise is to give you an opportunity to develop a capability statement for your own use.

STEPS	ACTION
1	Working with your colleagues, brainstorm key components of your company's capabilities.
2	Discuss these points and use them to develop an effective capability statement, about 100-200 words.
3	Refine the statement to make it suitable for presentation. Record it on audio tape and review.
4	Practise and amend as needed.

CONCLUDE

Concluding the call includes the following:

STEPS	ACTION
Summarise and check	Summarise any information you may have gained during the phone call. Confirm the appointment and set a time and place. Repeat the appointment, state what you will be covering, who will be attending, your phone number in case of any changes, and say that you will confirm in writing.
Recommend and check	Thank the prospect and express enthusiasm about the meeting.

CALL 24 HOURS BEFORE

Ring the day before to confirm the appointment and check directions etc.

THE NON-APPOINTMENTS

If you have done your target marketing properly, your prospect will probably have need or interest in your product at sometime or another. Ask when you could call back in a few months time to check their situation. Agree when you can call back, log this information in your tracking system. Most people are both flattered and impressed when you remember and call them back on the allotted date. Keep the real 'no thank yous' on a mailing list and keep chipping away.

Cold-calling blues

Your long-term success in sales will depend on your ability to locate, attract and develop new leads, in other words, prospecting. And that usually means 'cold-calling'!

There are few parts of the sales process that are so vital, and yet so emotive as the 'cold-call.' However, with planning you can make things a little easier.

With this approach – you always achieve something positive – even if you don't get an appointment first time around. You will get your name and details in the prospect's file, and make an impression on the prospect that marks you as a professional and trustworthy individual.

Even if you discover that the prospect genuinely has no need for your products or services at this time, the experience will leave him open to other sales calls. I call this approach, **warm-calling**, because when you speak to the prospect you are prepared and they should have a need, use or interest in your products and/or services and they may well have heard of you and be expecting your call.

Reasons for cold-calling blues

Most salespeople do not prospect enough. Here are some of the reasons why.

1. POOR ORGANISATION

- Energy diverted into non-critical areas (eg paperwork).
- Too much preparation and planning – not enough action.
- Over complicates process – too much jargon, etc.
- No system for tracking and following up on calls.

2. LOW SELF-ESTEEM

- Does not relate sales success to the spade work of prospecting – poor activity goals or too many.

- Takes themselves (or cold-calling) too seriously.

- Considers telephone prospecting 'unprofessional' or belittling.

- Poor self-image or does not see themselves as a salesperson.

- Hesitation due to seniority or manner of person.

- Gets too emotionally involved – takes rejection personally.

- Lack of support from others to aid self-motivation.

3. LOW SKILL LEVEL

- Prefers face-to-face meetings and contacts.

- Lacks telephone skills.

- Difficulty in getting through to contacts.

- Lacks lists or contacts.

- Unaware of potential benefits/conversion ratios.

4. NEGATIVE ATTITUDE

- Negative attitude 'Nobody's interested...'

- Uncomfortable as feels this is obtrusive.

- Easily distracted from telephone work.

- Excuses, excuses – always an excuse, never a reason.

- Problem focused – always finds something that won't work.

Which of the above statements apply to you?

Solutions to the cold-calling blues

1. ORGANISATION

- Set fixed times aside every day/week and do nothing else.

- Do not waste time in too much preparation – just get stuck in.

- Use a simple one page per day diary or computer database to remind you of call-backs.

2. SELF-ESTEEM

- Trace your call/appointment ration over a few weeks.

- Work in a group with a colleague when cold-calling.

- Make it fun: reward yourself with a cake or a drink when you reach a certain number of calls.

- Make the first and last call to a good customer – remind yourself of past successes.

- Act with enthusiasm.

- Introduce some friendly competition – either against your own goals or relative to your colleagues.

- Don't take it personally.

- Make a hundred calls!

- Set realistic objectives.

3. SKILLS

- Learn how: seek advice and listen to colleagues.

- Role-play or record and review your calls.

- Write word for word key questions and phrases and use as a 'prompt' sheet.

4. NEGATIVE ATTITUDES

- Positive self-talk.

- Act positive – keep busy.

- Avoid negative people and situations.

- Focus on small successes – finding people in, etc.

- Don't make excuses.

- Remember, the only way you can fail is by not making enough calls or not trying hard enough; giving up too soon.

SCHEDULE A 'COLD-CALLING' HOUR EVERY DAY

- Telephoning for appointments by making cold-calls is usually the least favourite activity of most salespeople, especially if you have not done it before or consistently (which is probably about 90 per cent of salespeople – they only do it when they have to!) However, if you resolve to make time every day for an intensive one-hour telephone cold-calling you can fill up your diary with appointments.

- In an hour's cold-calling you can probably make between 20-30 calls, only half of which will speak to you or be in, and only about a third of those will give you an appointment – but that's OK – it's all you need. Four appointments a day is probably more than you can handle if you are also getting some referrals, ongoing appointments and new leads. Two to three appointments a day, every day, will allow you to build a productive sales pipeline in a matter of weeks.

'Warm-calling': A three-step method to increase your sales

'Warm-calling' is an approach that aims to increase your success ratio.

Step 1: The target list

Establish and identify your target markets. It doesn't matter what you sell or to whom, if you don't identify those prospects most likely to buy them you are wasting the majority of your selling time.

To identify your target market create a profile of your perfect customer. If you are selling to individuals, your profile might include: age, sex, marital status, number of children, own or rent home, type of car, occupation, income, etc. If you sell business to business, your profile would include: company size, annual sales or revenues, industry, type of company, length of time in business, form of ownership, etc.

Define your ideal customer

Make some notes under the following heading and uncover your best prospects.

My ideal customer may be located within the following geographical area:

_____

_____

_____

My ideal customer may be this size of organisation:

_____

_____

_____

My ideal customer may have this attitude towards life or my product/ service:

_____

_____

_____

My ideal customer will be of the following age, sex, social status, etc:

_____

_____

_____

My ideal customer will consider the following to be important:

_____

_____

_____

My ideal customer may have the following problems:

_____

_____

_____

My ideal customer may have these personal characteristics or ambitions:

_____

_____

_____

Sources where I can identify or locate ideal prospects:

_____

_____

_____

Once you have created a customer profile, then you can begin comparing the world of prospects against it to determine smaller groups who are more likely to buy your specific product. You must then prioritise these prospects. Which have greater potential or could be sold to quicker? Which could give you the most referrals? List them by priority, starting with the highest and going to the lowest. At this point all you have are priority groups of prospects. Take time to locate your true prospects, it's worth the effort.

Step 2: The letter

Now that you have a solid prospect list you need to develop an introductory sales letter that 1) introduces the prospect to the benefits of doing business with you and 2) prepares him or her for your contact. The first paragraph is your attention grabber. Make statements or ask questions that hit the basic buying motives. (Most sales automation programmes have sample letters that you can customise and there are many books on the market with sample letters for you to use.) First determine the buying motives of your profiled customer. Motives can be convenience, ego or status, peer pressure, enjoyment or happiness, peace of mind, and time or money savings. Examples of opening statements or questions might be:

- Would you like to increase sales by 50 per cent?
- Small companies just like yours are saving thousands of pounds a year!
- Everyone is getting involved!
- Are you prepared to lose everything?
- Would you like your company to be number one?
- You could be making twice the profit in half the time!

Each opener hits a basic buying motive and should make the prospect read on. The balance of the first paragraph should support the statement and explain how you can help the prospect achieve the results mentioned in the opener. Keep it brief. Do not give the reader too much detail. Make your offer sound good but not beyond belief.

In the next paragraph ask for action or inform the prospect of the next step: a telephone call to set an appointment, class or seminar etc. If you will be following the letter with a telephone call, indicate approximately the day and date you will call. Research has shown that people will remember you and your letter better if there is a specific date set for your call.

Letters can be made more personal when signed either 'With Warm Regards' or just 'Warm Regards'. Also these letters seem to be more successful if you add a PS at the bottom of the page. The PS should hit the same benefit you presented in the opening paragraph.

Keep the letter to one page. Include a business card but no brochures, literature or flyers. These give the reader the opportunity to pre-judge your product or service without you there to explain and answer questions.

Step 3: The telephone call

Follow your letter with a telephone call, even if you don't indicate you will in the letter. Your telephone call has two purposes: to inform and to generate action. If, in your letter, you stated a day that you would call, make sure that you call on that day. The call should be brief and to the point. Again we break the call into three parts: the introduction, benefit statements and request for action.

PART 1

Introduce yourself and the company you represent. Mention why you have called and ask if he/she has a few minutes to speak. If he does not, ask for a more convenient time to call back. If he does have time to talk, continue on to the benefit statement.

PART 2

Repeat the benefit statement from the beginning of your introductory letter. Continue by briefly informing the prospect of how you will bring about this benefit. Then move on to the request for action.

PART 3

Make a confident request for action and expect to hear an objection or stall, 'We wouldn't be interested' or 'We're really busy, why don't you give us a call in 30 days.' If you can get by this objection, you will succeed about 90 per cent of the time. Be friendly and courteous, but persistent. Emphasise the benefits and keep asking for action.

When you have concluded the telephone call, whether you got the action requested or not, mail the prospect a thank-you note. (Stock thank-you notes are okay, personalised or company notes are much more professional.) If you have an appointment or they are attending something, reinforce the date and time in your thank-you note. Send along a business card, in case they lost the last one. If you did not get the requested action, reinforce your benefit statement and add a second one. Tell the prospect that you believe you have something that is truly beneficial and that you will stay in touch.

These three steps will ensure that you have all the prospects you need and that you are in front of qualified prospects more often. If you approach your appointment and presentation with the same structure and do an effective job of follow-up, you will increase your volume of appointments. Give yourself time to get used to the system and to build your prospect base. It takes time and effort, but will pay off in less wasted selling time and more sales to qualified buyers.

EXERCISE: TELEPHONE SCRIPT

Using the following as a template, plan out your ideas for gaining appointments by telephone:

(Points 1-3 are for dealing with an assistant.)

1 Introduce yourself

_____

_____

_____

2 Ask for assistance in achieving your objective

_____

_____

_____

3 Ask an indirect question requesting the person with whom you want to speak

_____

_____

_____

4 Confirm that you are speaking to the decision maker

_____

_____

_____

5 Tell them exactly why you are calling

_____

_____

_____

6 Make a friendly remark

_____

_____

_____

7 Stress a benefit

_____

_____

_____

8 Ask a question

_____

_____

_____

9 Make the pitch – a 30 second explanation of your product or service, highlighting the benefit to the prospect

_____

_____

_____

10 Attempt a trial close

_____

_____

_____

11 Answer and expand questions

_____

_____

_____

12 Ask for commitment (close)

_____

_____

_____

13 Summarise and express thanks

_____

_____

_____

Pre-determine your appointment times

Another very powerful technique is to plan your day's activities and appointments as a blueprint, and then slot the names and details in later. For instance, if your average call takes 45 minutes to an hour, and your normal calls are less than 30 minutes apart (if they aren't then look at how you are scheduling and planning your calls). Here is a typical day's blueprint:

9-10 am   Cold-calling hour

10.30 am   1st appointment

12.00 pm   2nd appointment

2.00 pm   3rd appointment (this could mean slightly more travelling time as you have lunchtime to get there)

3.30 pm   4th appointment

5.00 pm   Finish call sheets and telephone or return to the office.

If your sales calls are shorter or closer together then of course you can fit in five, six, or maybe eight or nine calls. Any more than about eight and the call time is so short and the selling opportunity so brief that you may end up being more efficient than effective.

Ideal appointment times

Start taking charge of your prospecting by putting an 'X' against the times that you would like to fill with an appointment:

TIMES	MON	TUES	WED	THUR	FRI
9					
10					
11					
12					
1					
2					
3					
4					

5					

Example call

Prospecting call structure

SALESPERSON	CUSTOMER
Good morning, Mr X?	Yes
Good morning, my name is .... and I'm calling from XXX, I understand that you are the Senior Partner, is that correct?	Yes, that's right
Good! Well, the reason I'm calling is to introduce myself and let you know of some new facilities that we have recently introduced regarding xyz Ltd, which I don't think you are aware of..? *or* The reason I'm calling is to introduce myself and see if it is possible to see you to tell you about our new, interesting and different approach to xyz Ltd.	No, I don't think so...

Prospecting call structure *continued*

SALESPERSON	CUSTOMER
What service do you currently use with regard to xyz Ltd?	We offer...
I see, good (whatever they say). As I mentioned, we have a slightly different approach to XYZ Ltd that I think will be of interest... it will actually allow you to...	Fine, what time?
I wonder if I could call in to meet you and introduce myself and have a brief chat about your business? How does Tuesday week look?	Fine, what time? *or* That's impossible, because...
Handle objection	
Re-close for appointment	Gain appointment or log as call-back

Prospect tracking

There is a lot more to gaining appointments effectively on the telephone than simply having 'the gift of the gab' and picking up the telephone every now and then. If you are to be successful and consistent in gaining appointments, you need to have a system. This system is a way of tracking call-backs, people you have spoken to, recording information and measuring activity levels. It is often known as organised persistence. Organisation without persistence is not that effective, and persistence without organisation is usually doomed to failure. The two combined can create an effective and very easy method of generating new business leads.

Call-back system

As the volume of your telephone calls rises, you will find it increasingly difficult to remember who you have spoken to and when you have agreed to call them back. If you consider that at least 50 per cent of the people that you try and contact will not be in or available and therefore will need to be called back, you will soon see that calling people back efficiently is an essential part of any good prospecting system.

If you have the benefit of a contacts management computer database, this will usually take care of this particular task for you. Call-back dates can be scheduled in the diary section and then by entering the system on a particular date, the system automatically produces the call-backs for the day or week. If, however, you are using more low-tech methods, these can be just as successful and just as easy to use.

Whilst there are proprietary systems available, two of the most effective ways can actually be created using standard stationery items. By combining an ordinary record card system with a one day per page diary it is possible to create a list of people to call back for any particular date in the year. For example, if we called someone today, who then asked or we agreed a call-back for three or four months time, we could turn to the relevant page in our diary, put their name, company and telephone number and then not worry about trying to remember it. In a few months time when we turn to that page we will then find a list has been built up of people to call that day.

As two of the most demotivating things in sales are not knowing what to do, or not having enough to do, this simple mechanism can ensure that we don't fall into this trap. Every time somebody is not around, not available, or simply does not need to see us at this point in time, we can log a future call-back in our one day per page diary. An alternative method is to use an A4 file, with a one to 31 section and a January to December series of sections.

Customer data sheets are then created using an A4 page, and inserted into the appropriate day and month in the future. In this way sheets can be moved around the file, according to when the customer needs to be called back.

Record keeping

It is essential to keep brief but useful notes on each call that we make. Many salespeople find that a very effective method is by using an 8" by 5" index card, with the organisation's details on the front and a simple one line summary of what has been discussed. This is usually all that is needed to jog our memories the next time we pick up that card to call the customer.

If you deal with larger accounts or a fewer number of prospects, you may choose to keep more detailed information on each individual prospect. Whichever you choose it is important to remember that good record keeping is important. This is important for your own use and for the company and also if anyone else takes over those prospects or territory. Another advantage of good record keeping is that when you contact your prospect you can relate back information that you discussed at the time. This nearly always impresses the prospect.

On the telephone of course we do not have any visual communication, we cannot actually see the other person or be seen ourselves. This means that voice tone and the words that we use become twice as important as they would do in normal conversation. Indeed, our voice tone and how we sound is how the customer and other people judge our sincerity, honesty, professionalism, helpfulness, efficiency and knowledge. What we actually say, the singular words that we use are either not heard or not that important. It is the voice tone that allows us to project the image that we want to achieve.

Indeed, this is what happens when we are trying to sell something over the telephone, and they may quickly tell us that it is not convenient. An example of a good series of qualification questions would be something like 'Hello, is that Mr Jones?... Are you the computer manager?... And would you be the right person to talk to about network support?'

Appointments – application assignments

The following exercises will help you transfer the skills and methods from this section into your work.

1. Design a form that you might use to track the number of dials, connected calls and appointments. Make sure that it is quick to complete and yet will allow you to track your conversion ratio and follow-up calls.

2. Start a prospecting file of company names, business cards, articles, adverts etc that can be used as names to call.

3. For one whole week, spend at least one hour a day cold or warm calling.

4. Have a 'Telephone Attack Day'. Working with a colleague, making it easier to stay motivated. Spend one whole day telephoning for appointments.

5. Use a whiteboard to track and log appointments and call-backs, so that you can literally keep prospecting in focus!

6. Talk to managers and secretaries in your own organisation – how do other companies get through to them; what works in terms of other companies selling to your organisation?

7. Make enquiries about a number of business products where you have some need eg photocopying, graphic design etc. Assess how well they follow-up and contact you to try and gain an appointment.

PART THREE

ACHIEVING BETTER SALES RESULTS ON THE TELEPHONE

How to get even better sales results	126
Customer focus	129
Selling and customer service	131
An introduction to selling on the telephone	132
Structuring a sales call	137
Preparation, organisation and planning	140
Converting incoming calls into sales	145
Outgoing calls – working a list	148
Personal organisation	152
Activities levels	154
Voice projection	158
The sales call	160
The voice that sells	161
Telephone sales questioning techniques	163
Features and benefits (FAB)	176
Developing FAB statements	178
People buy for different reasons	180
Handling objections and questions	183
Overcoming objections	186
Closing the sale	189
Ending the call	193
Telephone selling – application assignments	195

ACHIEVING BETTER SALES RESULTS ON THE TELEPHONE

How to get even better sales results

There are several crucial differences to communicating or selling by telephone rather than by face-to-face. For instance, using the telephone can be slightly obtrusive, especially if you are calling people in their homes, it may also be rather less impersonal and difficult to read the other person's 'body language'.

The way that we can deal with these differences is to learn a series of sharpened techniques that can allow us to compensate for them, and perhaps even use them to our own advantage.

Qualities of a successful telemarketer

The main role of a telemarketing executive is to generate sales, either by converting in-bound enquiries or outbound calling. In some, the objective is to secure appointments for a direct sales force.

There is no such thing as a product of service that will sell itself as effectively as it can be sold by a good salesperson. A client will always 'buy' the telemarketer before he/she buys the product/service. Therefore an effective telemarketing department is a crucial part of any successful organisation, which in turn is only as good as the personalities within it.

Personal qualities

There are key personal qualities that are essential for telephone work:

- self-motivation
- determination
- enthusiasm
- organisation
- sense of humour
- professionalism
- confidence
- flexibility
- quick-thinking
- thick-skinned, and many more.

People buy people first, and everything else second.

The power of the telephone

The telephone may seem to be a routine piece of equipment but using it effectively in business is a vital skill.

The telephone is a vital communication link, without which many businesses would simply not survive, or even exist.

How quickly the telephone is answered, the initial greeting, and how the person sounds all create an impression in the mind of the caller. Many callers judge the whole company and all its products by the way their call is handled.

We can influence a customer to do business with our company by learning and applying a few simple rules of telephone sales technique. When we use the telephone professionally, we create the climate in which new customers want to do business with us, and existing customers continue to do business. Our job also becomes more interesting and rewarding as customers respond positively to a more professional approach.

Advantages and disadvantages of selling by telephone

ADVANTAGES

Timesaving: You can be making calls each day instead of wasting time travelling. You can reach an office anywhere in the country in a matter of seconds.

Anonymity: There is a degree anonymity when using the telephone. All that is perceptible is your voice and manner. This leaves you free to concentrate on communicating – and getting it right.

Appearance: On the telephone your appearance does not count. There is no way it can prejudice your chances of successful transaction. This does not mean that you should forget your appearance – if you look slovenly, you probably feel it. This can come across on the telephone as clearly as if you were sitting in the same room, to say nothing of the effect on those who have to work with you.

Inhibitions: You should be able to forget any inhibitions you may have, and become free to concentrate on the call.

Preparation: On an outbound call you can be physically and mentally prepared. Questions, objections and goals in mind – you make the call when you are ready.

DISADVANTAGES

Any disadvantages should easily be overcome by a good telemarketer who applies their training effectively.

No visuals: Because you cannot be seen by your customer, you must create a positive impression through your voice tone, words and mannerisms.

Time distortion: Time is premium on the telephone, and every second counts.

Personal contact: It is hard to beat personal contact in a business relationship and the telephone can distance the two parties involved. However, if it is used properly, there is a unique relationship that can be developed on the phone.

Telephone abuse: You must remember at all times that the telephone can present you in a bad light if used incorrectly. If you have ever spoken to somebody who is eating, smoking, chewing gum or coughing into the receiver, you will realise how the telephone amplifies noises that you are not aware of making. **DON'T DO IT!**

Customer focus

The best way to start when selling on the telephone is to consider the customer: their needs, preferences and emotions.

Develop a positive customer attitude

- Treat each and every customer as the most important person in your day.

- Do **NOT** think that a customer is an interruption to your work. He/she is the purpose of it. We are not doing them a favour by serving him/her... He/she is doing us a favour by giving us the opportunity to do so.

- Do **NOT** believe the customer is someone to argue with. Nobody ever won an argument with a customer... and if they did, they probably lost the customer.

Know your customer as well as your products

There are two areas that require knowledge in any sales solutions: the marketplace and the product. You must be obsessive in your desire to find out all you can on both subjects. Confidence and enthusiasm come through knowledge. No matter how good your sales technique is, you simply will not be able to sell effectively if you don't know the facts.

Know your product

With the knowledge of the product you can point out the features and benefits of your service and answer objections and queries accurately, without hesitation. Below is a checklist which includes the main points you should research about the company or products.

Good product knowledge gives you and your customer confidence.

- Who are the directors and management team of your company?

- What literature and brochures are available about the service or products?

- What offers and new product launches are planned by your company (and your competitors)?

- Learn the unique features and benefits of the service.

- Read the trade and business press.

Selling and customer service

Service

Service is the feeling (good or poor) that a service recipient has with the service-giver or salesperson.

If your business is competitive, it is possible to find firms with comparable products, prices and quality. In this situation the business will go to the organisation that appears to provide the best products **AND** *personal service.*

Personal service needs to start right inside your own office. Giving good service to each other, whether at home or at work, is really about giving people a sense of well-being.

Satisfying customers is actually about meeting their needs. As a service giver, you are faced with the challenge of meeting their needs. You won't always be able to meet them all of course, indeed on occasions you may be stretched to meet **ANY** of their needs.

Focusing on individual needs in this way could certainly upset a few routines and may be rather more demanding. On balance though, you will have a greater sense of fulfilment at the end of each day.

Good service is meeting people's needs in a way that exceeds their expectations.

Your aim must be to give customers exceptional personal service, at all times.

An introduction to selling on the telephone

Selling

Selling is about helping people buy.

The more you try and 'sell', the less people will be likely to buy, or return, or hold your organisation in high-esteem.

In addition, the limitations of the telephone mean that you are less convincing, less trusted and have less time. Therefore, don't sell, help people make good buying decisions.

People buy for a variety of reasons, so it is important that you are aware of these potential factors so you can adapt the call to meet particular needs.

People do not buy a product or a service, they buy what a product or service will do for them – in other words, what benefits can your product or service offer to encourage people to buy?

To find out, you need to consider various points.

PEOPLE BUY WHAT THEY WANT

The average person goes through the 'Wish-Want-Need' thinking process before buying a special purchase.

'I *wish* I had that.'

'I *want* that.'

'I *need* that.'

PEOPLE BUY WHAT PRODUCTS CAN DO FOR THEM

Most products have many fine features but the customer buys what he/she can get out of the product. You need to translate the features to benefits.

> *The fact is that you cannot 'sell' on the telephone – your purpose is to help people buy.*

KNOW WHAT YOUR PRODUCT CAN DO

Knowing the features or selling points that together make up your product is not the same thing as knowing the application for your product. Complete product knowledge is both.

> The first sale you make is to yourself.

BELIEVE IN WHAT YOU ARE SELLING

One of the most difficult tasks for anybody must be to sell something that they believe is bad or not good enough. Most people, if faced with the situation find selling an impossible task, because they feel they have to lie.

If you believe in what you are selling, people around you will believe in it. You don't have to 'love' your product, just be **ENTHUSIASTIC** about it. Enthusiasm is contagious.

Know what your customer wants done

Different customers often want different things from the same product – in other words, match what your product can do with that which the customer wants or needs, and you have a benefit.

SHARE THE CUSTOMER'S POINT OF VIEW

Think about the customer's needs/problems as though they were your own. Visualise the situation that they may be facing. Selling is helping a customer to buy what they want to buy – **BENEFITS**.

PEOPLE BUY PEOPLE FIRST

- The customer buys you before he/she buys your product.
- To be successful at selling you must sell yourself first.
- People like people to like them – find something in common with the customer.
- People like people to agree with them.
- People like people who are interested in them.

Helping people buy

Contrast these two examples from a mobile phone sales enquiry:

THE WRONG WAY

Salesperson   How may I help you?

Customer   I am interested in finding out more about the offer which I saw advertised in the paper yesterday...

Salesperson   The new Talkphone A Plan and flip-phone?

Customer   Yes, that's right.

Salesperson   Yes, this is an excellent offer, the flip-phone is great, in fact I use one myself (probably not true) it has loads of super features, automatic redials, 100 number memory...

Customer   (Interrupting) I see, how about the tariffs...?

Salesperson	Yes, er... tariffs?... (sounding unsure) ...yes they are good too, there are four different ones – the first one is called A1 and the off-peak rate is... (now reading from brochure), peak rate is ...and you get ...minutes free every month, plus we have a special offer running at the moment which gives you... on the other hand A2 has a rate of...
	(some minutes later)
	Which tariff do you want?
Customer	er... I'm not sure really...
Salesperson	OK, well, most people go for the A1 plan...shall I take your order now?
Customer	No, I need to have a think about this...
Salesperson	*(now into closing mode)* Well, this offer is only available for a limited time and we might run out of stock... would you like me to hold one and call you back later on today?
Customer	No, that's OK, I'll call you back when I'm ready.

THE RIGHT WAY

Salesperson	Good morning, how may I help you?
Customer	I'm interested in finding out more about your offer I saw advertised in the paper yesterday...
Salesperson	Yes, of course, my name is John, may I take your name?
Customer	Yes, David Jones.

Salesperson	Thank you Mr Jones, first I need to ask you a few quick questions and then tell you a bit more about what we can offer.
Customer	OK.
Salesperson	How often do you estimate you will be using a mobile phone and is it for personal or business use?
Customer	Mainly personal, so that I can keep in touch with people while I'm travelling and just for general convenience.
Salesperson	Would you expect to use your phone for more than ten minutes a day, on average?
Customer	No, I don't think so.
Salesperson	OK, that's fine. I would recommend the flip-phone featured in the advert with the A3 call plan. This allows you the lowest monthly rental together with free off-peak calls at evenings and weekends. Have you used a mobile phone before? (*Asking a question keeps the sales person in control.*)
Customer	No, never.
Salesperson	OK that's fine, the flip-phone has lots of features and is very easy to use, very neat and compact so that you can carry it with you all the time, and we offer a 24 hour customer help-line, which means that if you ever have a question or query, we are just a call away. It is a very popular telephone. Do you have any questions?

Customer	Yes, are there any other costs apart from the monthly line rental and call costs?
Salesperson	Yes, only one... a one-off connection charge of £... which is standard on all of our telephones...
	How soon were you thinking of getting your phone?
Customer	Well, as soon as possible really.
Salesperson	OK, I will just check to see if we have any in stock...
	Yes, we have those in stock. If you would like me to, I can take your order by telephone today, using a credit card and you will receive your new phone and start-up pack within 48 hours. You should be able to start using it the same day you receive it.
	Would you like me to arrange that for you now?

Structuring a sales call

Due to the volume of telephone contacts that you can take or make during the day it is vital to be properly organised, well prepared and have a definite plan or objective.

Additionally, as the volume of contacts increases, you are likely to receive a much higher level of rejection than you might normally do in face-to-face selling. You may also have far more people to contact and have far greater pressures in terms of constant activity. This means that you cannot afford the luxury of simply drifting from one call to another. You need to have a definite positive, proactive approach. Particularly if you are reacting to incoming calls, you must be ready to answer questions, be organised and prepared to close sales effectively.

Opening the sales call

We only have one chance to make a good first impression. In face-to-face communications this first impression may be four or five minutes. Using the telephone, this first impression is probably the first 30 to 40 seconds. We need to make a very planned, precise and careful use of the opening part of a telephone conversation if we are going to be able to continue it through to the second half of the call and gain some further commitment and perhaps make a sale.

Refer to Part One on how your opening should sound.

Building the sale

As time is limited on the telephone we need to quickly move in to what is known as building or creating the sale. Once initial information and qualification of the customer has taken place, we need to quickly present our solution, benefits and proposals.

Your questioning techniques should be precise and well-planned. Use active listening to further create sales opportunities.

One of the most important things you may be able to do on the telephone is make it easier for customers to do business. If we have a strong product or service, or well-defined features and benefits, then by making ourselves sound attractive, confident and professional we can persuade the customer by simply making the decision-making process as easy and as straightforward as possible.

Gaining commitment

In most cases, however, people will need some assistance in helping them make a buying decision. We can do this in several ways. The first is to become very aware of buying signals and there are a whole series of different things that we can look and listen for which allow us to gauge the customer's buying readiness. We can then follow this with trial or test closing questions. These act to confirm our suspicions about whether the customer is ready to make a decision to buy, or a commitment to proceed further.

At some point in this process you are likely to gather some objections or questions that still remain in the mind of the customer which they need to have answered before they proceed with any more commitment or agreement. By proactively sitting down and thinking about the kind of objections that we are likely to encounter, we can then prepare definite answers to these and be more successful in closing and confirming sales.

The final stage of this process is of course to close the sale, ask for some form of commitment or agreement and confirm and follow this up on a positive and a proactive and reassuring manner.

The five steps to selling successfully by telephone are good preparation, strong call opening, positive building of benefits, gaining commitment and closing.

Preparation, organisation and planning

The sales process – at a glance

PLAN THE CALL

- Preparation
- Set call objectives

OPEN THE CALL

- Use structure/script
- Handle initial 'put-offs'
- Qualify interest level

BUILD OPPORTUNITIES

- Establish rapport
- Identify problems/needs
- Identify buying preferences

PRESENT OPTIONS

- Offer solutions/options
- Sell benefits
- Handle questions

CLOSE THE SALE

- Handle objections
- Ask for commitment
- Confirm details

The sales process

These three words often strike fear into the heart of many otherwise completely rational salespeople. It is somehow thought that by better planning, becoming organised or taking time out to be better prepared we are going to loose some of our elusive intuitiveness, or responsiveness. There is a great deal of benefit in becoming much more proactive in planning. This is important particularly on the telephone. An average telephone sales person may speak to anything between 50 to 350 different customers in a single day. This can mean a huge drain on time and resources, not to mention stress! By becoming better organised we can actually become better placed to sell.

Being organised and prepared may mean a number of things. It may simply mean having a pen and paper to hand whenever the telephone rings. It may mean knowing our computer software extremely well so that we avoid waiting time when looking up or entering customer information. It means knowing our products extremely well. It means knowing our customers even better, and pre-empting some of their commonly asked questions so that we can be prepared with the right answers.

It also means being particularly planned and structured using a series of prompts as required. These can dramatically increase our effectiveness over the telephone, and are aids not available to face-to-face salespeople. As the customer cannot see you, we are able to use information in front of us to help guide us through the sales conversation. In many sophisticated and advanced applications of telephone selling, salespeople are guided by on screen prompts from an interactive computer screen which guides them through each stage of the conversation depending on the points the customer makes.

Help people get what they want

In defining the image of ourselves as salespeople, it is important to understand that we don't sell anything to anybody. Rather we sell goods and services that don't come back to customers that do! Your role as a professional sales person is to help people get what it is that they want. This may be the solution to the problem that your product or service offers. If may also be the feeling of dealing with a professional or quality organisation. It may be the feeling of getting a special offer or a special price on something and therefore saving money. The way that we help people get this feeling and these solutions is known as professional selling.

Why do people buy what they buy?

This is an important question to understand as part of the preparation for selling successfully, or more successfully. If we understand why people buy what they buy, we can be more deliberate in presenting our information to the best effect. Behavioural psychologists and consumer specialists who have studied consumer psychology have identified two or three major reasons why people buy what they buy.

1. IMPROVEMENT

Clearly people buy to improve their situation. They try to overcome a dissatisfaction or a need. You may already have a good stereo for example, but have a general dissatisfaction with a certain aspect of it. Something may happen to then trigger that dissatisfaction into a buying action. This could be that you happen to see a particular special offer, and this prompts you to take action. It may be on talking to friends that you realise just how out of date your system is.

2. DESIRES

As well as buying what we need, we also buy what we want. And we all want a great many things! As well as buying a simple solution to a problem, people are also buying how it feels or how they believe it will feel to own that particular product or service. For example, the reason why one customer chooses consciously one bank over another may be largely be down to the feeling or instinct to become a customer in that particular organisation. This is what much of modern advertising strives to achieve. By positioning brands, emotions, perspectives, and opinions in our minds over a period of time buying influences can be made.

3. PEOPLE ALSO BUY FOR THEIR OWN REASONS

It is important to remember that regardless of the features or benefits we believe exist in our product or service, people will ultimately buy for their own reasons. As the old saying goes, the customer is always right. For example, if a customer wants to buy a new computer system from one company because it prefers the shape of the outside case, then of course he or she is completely right in their judgement. And as quality and service standards have increased dramatically over the last few years these apparent differences in detail have become much smaller. This means that people's reasons for buying can sometimes be very subtle and very small indeed. Indeed, one of the major differences between why a customer buys product A or product B can be the sales or customer service person they are dealing with at the point of contact. That means you!

How people buy

Once you have begun to understand more about why people buy, you need to understand how they arrive at these buying decisions. There are two vital rules that need to be borne in mind when trying to sell successfully.

> If you say it they will question it. If they say it, they will believe it.

1. PEOPLE BUY ON EMOTION AND JUSTIFY WITH FACT

The best way to highlight this is to think of something, perhaps a major purchase, that you have made recently. Consider for a moment how you went about making your buying decision. How did you weigh the pros and cons? Did you buy on impulse? Was it a combination of the two? Have you ever encountered a situation where you have bought something largely on impulse or a whim and then found yourself justifying the need for that particular item?

Think also about some of the phrases that people use when they need something, for example 'I really need a new suit'. Do they really need a new suit? Or is it rather something that they would like to have. Your goal as a sales person is to make people *want* what you have to sell, that is to trigger the emotions of buying, but at the same time *give* the people the reasons to *justify logically and rationally* the purchase decision to themselves. This is true if you are selling consumer items or expensive business solutions to corporate organisations. The process is identical.

2. FIND THE HOT BUTTON

This simply means that of all the features and benefits, all the needs and wants and all the reasons to buy that may exist, people buy for only one or two major reasons. In many cases it may be one single factor, sometimes referred to as the hot button, that will be the overriding criteria in making a buying decision. For example, if you are buying a car it might be economy or style. If you are buying a house it might be the location, size or facilities. It is essential to try and anticipate and identify the customer's hot buttons. In many cases we can discover this by simply asking for it. It some cases quite directly. In other cases, the customers may not be aware of the hot button themselves, and therefore we need to have the skills and confidence to guide them carefully to uncover their most important factors in making a buying decision.

Converting incoming calls into sales

Incoming calls are different only from outgoing calls in who actually initiates the telephone call in the first instance. Where you have initiated the call, then you need to be slightly more assertive and slightly more prepared when introducing yourself. In both types of calls the call structure is vital, and remains unchanged throughout the call.

A common fallacy is that if the call is incoming, then you have less control over the conversation. This is not true, or rather need not be true. You need to quickly gain control of the telephone conversation regardless of whether it is incoming or outgoing. If it is incoming something must have prompted the customer to make the call. Your job is to find out what that is and to build on that as quickly and as efficiently as possible.

Incoming calls quick qualification

It is safe to assume that the customer or prospect telephoning will have some level of buying interest, urgency and desire. The very first thing that we should do therefore, is to be ready to qualify and quantify what is of interest and urgent. We can often tell this by the questions asked, the tone of voice and the willingness to work with the salesperson as they ask our questions.

Many successful salespeople find it useful to put the customer or the prospect in one of three or four different categories. By doing this they can then vary their approach which suits the customer's level of buying readiness.

Four such categories are:

1. tyre kicker
2. suspect
3. prospect
4. hot potato.

TYRE KICKER

A tyre kicker is one of those brochure collectors or catalogue browsers that go round car showrooms to make sure they are up-to-date on the latest prices and specifications. They probably won't change their car any more frequently than you or me, but just enjoy the process of looking. Any marketing or advertising campaign will always generate a response from these type of individuals. They are always looking for a better offer, they are always looking for more information and frequently looking for opportunities to show how much they know about something. It is important that we deal with this type of customer and prospect professionally and politely because one day they will buy. We must guard though against them taking too much of our time until we have qualified when, what and where they are going to buy.

SUSPECT

This is the next level of buying readiness and is someone who we may suspect has a vague need or intent to purchase from us or a similar competitor. They are at the process of 'just looking', and are probably at the stage of gathering background or general information to help them ask more pertinent questions and make a more informed approach. This is particularly true of organisations or company purchases. It also applies to us as individuals when we are making a major purchase. For example, many of us will keep our eye out in the shop or papers when we are considering buying something often a long time before we can afford it or are ready to make a decision. These people need to be given due respect and professionalism but the time to deal with them is in the future and we must do everything we can to make sure they are followed up effectively using a professional call-back system.

PROSPECT

A prospect is somebody who has a specific, clearly identified need with a timescale with which to proceed. This doesn't mean that the need or the timescale may change, it just means they already have it currently assessed. Instead of vague wants and desires they have *specific* wants and desires. You may sense from this individual that they have a very good knowledge of your competitors and what else is available. This is definitely a good sign and shows that they have been spending time and attention on this matter. These people are definitely worth a good investment in time and are more easily prompted to make a decision and can be impressed by good quality sales advice and high level customer service.

HOT POTATO

A hot potato is also known as a self-actualising buyer. This is somebody who knows what they want, have made up their mind more or less about the model, make, specification and all they have to decide is who they want to buy it from. The reason it is nicknamed a hot potato is because the only thing you can do with a hot potato is, of course, drop it. They need to be handled carefully, efficiently and most of all brusquely because they are probably just about to buy.

Outgoing calls – working a list

Once you have assembled and identified good sources of prospects on an ongoing basis, you need to approach this list of prospects with a view to generating qualified leads, sales opportunities and close the business. In most cases this is referred to as 'Working a list'. It is not uncommon to have a large list of prospects that you work through on a systematic basis. Indeed, many top telesales professionals have proved to be extremely successful. Resist the temptation to dip into a prospect list and pick out what you think are the richest or choicest chunks, instead approach it in a methodical manner, looking to work the list from beginning to end.

Following are the four steps.

1. Define your ideal customer

It is important that you make sure that your prospects are ones that have the very best chance of converting into customers. The easiest and fastest way of doing this is looking at who your customers are now, and using this profile to help you detect likely prospects. Begin by profiling your ideal customer, basing it on your current bank of customers. If you sell to businesses, the considerations may be the geographic location of the business, (although this is less important on the telephone), the size and nature of the organisation, their structure, turnover, number of employees and so on. If you sell to consumers then geography may be important but so too will be past buying patterns, interests and so on. You may also need to consider the psychological aspects of prospects. That is, what is the attitude they have towards your product or service. For example, there is limited scope selling sports insurance to people who do not actively participate in any major sports.

2. Develop a good 'script'

It is important to recognise that scripting, or working from a series of prepared prompts or questions, is the single greatest thing you can do to improve your effectiveness in selling on the telephone, especially with out-bound calls.

You may find yourself disagreeing with this point or experiencing some resistance to the idea of using a 'canned' presentation. The difference is how you deliver your script. Obviously you use what you have written down as a series of prompts (rather than read it verbatim). A prompt sheet will serve to remind you of some well chosen phrases and terms, and allow you a degree of control (and flexibility) during the conversation. The reason for this is because you don't have to worry about what you need to say, rather you can concentrate on how you say it and more importantly what your customer is saying.

Many top telephone sales professionals regularly write and rewrite their sales 'script'. They will start a list with a brand new script and revise it and amend it as they work their way through it. Each time you make a call you can be finding out something new which will help you to make the next call much more effective.

3. Elimination

The secret of working a list is to eliminate temporarily the people that are not available and identify the cherries that are ripe for picking. The underlying philosophy of working through a prospect list is that a percentage of that list are looking for what you have to sell or offer right at this time. Your job as a telephone sales professional is simply to find them. If you have a list of a thousand people it might be only the first ten you phone or it might be the last ten you phone, you won't know until you have phoned them.

Move through a call systematically and thoroughly.

When a customer says 'no, I'm not interested', they really mean 'not today', or 'you haven't convinced me yet'.

So, as you go through the list it is important to make notes against each of the names. You can create your own code for this but simple terminology such as NA for not available. Other notes that you might like to make is C for a connected call, and then mark levels of interest with either one, two or three stars depending on how good a prospect you believe they are.

4. Persistence

There is no question that using the telephone to sell takes a great deal of skill and a large amount of persistence. Persistence allows you to keep going through a large number of the 'no thank yous' or 'not todays' that you may get as you work through your prospect list. Remember that you may speak to more people in a morning than most salespeople contact face-to-face in a week or a month. This level of rejection requires a great deal of confidence and persistence (or an outstanding sense of humour) on the part of the salesperson.

Understanding that the numbers that you dial are simply the means to the end is the important part of maintaining your activity level when working through a prospect list. Knowing your sales ratios can also be important. For example, if you know that when you dial 20 numbers, you will only realistically speak to ten people – the others being out or unavailable – then this will ensure that you do not get too despondent when you don't get through to everybody. Another key ratio to understand is that out of the ten people that you speak to only a couple may actually be mildly interested or curious as to what you are offering. This is not a rejection, this is simply the customer saying not today.

Making your sales target is largely about dialling enough telephone numbers.

Another successful skill that top telesales professionals have developed is the ability to rework a list the second or third time. We have a tendency to always think that the next list that we get hold of will somehow be better and more successful than the one we have. This may not always be true. It may actually be the case that one list is not any better or any worse than another. Once you have gone through a list you will probably have contacted about 40 or 50 per cent of the people on the list. This means that at least another half of the list has not been reached by you, and to disregard the list now is to throw away half its potential. Of the people that you actually spoke to or connected with, there may be 25 or 30 per cent who expressed no interest at the time but may do in the future.

A difference of three or four months or even three or four weeks may make a large difference in whether a prospect list is very successful or simply just average. This is why it is important to make clear notes on your list, because it can refer you to it again and again. One technique might be to swap lists with another colleague so that you work the second time on a different list but from the same source. This allows you to approach a list from the same source afresh, but in the same way maintaining the consistency that is so important when working through a list of prospects.

Personal organisation

Prospect tracking

Depending on your type of business it is probably very likely that you will need to contact the same prospect or customers several times before they make a buying decision. This facilitates the need for what is known as a prospect tracking system. This is sometimes known as a call-back system.

1. CALL-BACK SYSTEM

A call-back system is simply a method that you develop that will remind you who to call back and when, regardless of how long in the future they need to be contacted.

There are many sophisticated computer based systems available to do this task extremely well. You can get equally good results from simply using a one-day-per-page-diary. Simply enter in the name of the individual, company and telephone number under the relevant day which they have requested that you call them back. As you go through the days and weeks, the days will be added to so that when you turn over the page at the start of each morning you are already greeted by quite a long list of existing potential prospects ready and waiting for your call.

As Woody Allen once said 90 per cent of success is showing up. In selling, 90 per cent of success is making the sales call. The great majority of your competitors will not have the self-discipline, knowledge or motivation to maintain an active call-back system. They will be too busy working a list once and then rushing off to the next list. You, however, now understand the value and the benefit of developing a sound call-back system. Consider also that these particular customers – having spoken to you or received information from you once already – will be less resistant and more amenable to your call.

2. RECORD KEEPING

Brief but accurate records are vital. It is important to keep a record of each conversation and the key points of each customer. If you have access to a computer system it can make this particular facility very easy. However, try to avoid the temptation to keep more information than you need.

If you look at what you would keep if you had a record card system then that is perhaps what you should look to keep on the computer system. On the front of your record card you would have the basic information regarding that organisation or customer, name, address, telephone number, previous products purchased, areas of interest, category of interest and so on. On the back you would have three columns: date, activity and result. Activity would simply be a line or one sentence description of what happened plus a couple of words indicating the next action. In this way when you contact your customer again in the future you can actually refer back to points or dates where other things were discussed. This is extremely impressive to customers, particularly when it is a sign of efficiency rather than persistence.

Organised persistence

Organised persistence is the name given to the end result of keeping an accurate call back system with accurate record keeping. It will enable you to select and keep the very best prospects and customers and move with them as they develop their sales needs and requirements. Remember, some customers will buy very quickly and others may take much longer. Your job as a sales professional is to sell professionally and in a way which is in sympathy with how customers want to buy. We need to influence people and help them make quicker decisions, but at all times we need to be respectful to their buying criteria and procedure.

One of the things that many top sales professionals have found, particularly those selling ongoing products and services to businesses, is to stay in touch with existing customers and prospects. When a customer buys, once it is usually only a trial purchase. We need to keep in contact with those customers with something new, interesting or different on a regular basis. When you are selling to businesses 90 days is a normal business quarter and is seen as being neither too pushy, nor too infrequent to miss opportunities.

Activities levels

As mentioned already, selling by telephone is a numbers game, and no amount of scientific analysis of prospect or customer motivations can get away from this fact. The more calls you take or make, on an average basis, the more sales you make. Also, the more calls you make, the more effective you will become at selling on the telephone, and you will quickly improve. Occasionally you will meet salespeople who have an outstanding success rate from a low call rate. These people are more likely the exception than the rule, and operate either in a specialist field or have developed a highly skilled approach or have some specialist knowledge that allows this to be possible. There is nothing particularly complicated about setting sales activity levels other than you have to have sales goals.

1. DAILY SCHEDULES – OUTBOUND CALLING

The first place to start is by creating a realistic and workable daily schedule for yourself. Start off by making cold-calling or the most difficult prospecting call, a priority. Do this first. If nothing else you will then have it out of the way and you can progress to other calls. Divide your day into a series of one hour slots and allocate different types of calls to each of these one or two hour chunks. For example, you might have a session of cold-calling on new prospects you haven't contacted before, followed by a series of follow-up calls to people that you have spoken to or sent information to recently. You may then have another session for confirmation calls or closing calls to people from whom you are awaiting a decision. By dividing your day you can best prepare yourself, both physically and mentally to be as effective as possible. Each of these type of calls may take a different list, a different script and a slightly different approach. So, rather than jumping from one task to another set yourself a daily schedule and, or a weekly schedule where you will fit in four or five different types of calls. It is also important to schedule time for administration, paperwork and product knowledge.

In-bound call handling requires you to be mainly reactive. However, be sure to take time at regular intervals to fulfill any customer actions – call backs, etc.

2. GOAL SETTING

It is also important that you have clear sales goals. These should be goals in terms of value, that is, how much you actually want to sell in money terms (this may of course translate into how much commission you would like to earn) and also sales activity goals. Sales managers have found that the three things that de-motivate salespeople the most is not having enough to do, having too much to do and not knowing what to do. By setting realistic sales achievement and activity goals, we can avoid these particular pitfalls.

Your sales goals should be set perhaps per year, possibly each quarter, certainly each month, definitely each week and absolutely every day.

It is essential that you start each day with a very clear target for how many telephone outgoing calls, or incoming calls, that you should take or make every day. This target should then be reviewed and updated regularly, say every two or three months to make sure that it is still challenging and still driving you to reach your full potential. The actual number of calls that you may make can vary depending on your type of business, the number of potential prospects and your expectations as an organisation. There are some telephone sale people who regularly make 300 calls a day, others may only make 20 or 30. What is important is that you make sure that you are making enough.

3. CONVERSION RATIOS

In order for you to know how many telephone calls is enough, it is necessary for you to understand or identify your conversion ratio. This is the number of sales that you generate from a certain number of calls. To put it very simply, it means that it you want to make ten sales a day, and you know that for every ten calls that you make you will have one order, on average, then you now know how many calls you have to make to achieve your target.

Improving your sales conversation is one of the surest ways of being successful long-term.

You can further analyse your conversion ratio by breaking it down from cold call to prospect and then prospect to proposal. In this way you can identify where your strengths and weaknesses are in your presentation. For example if you find that you are having a great deal of success getting through to potential prospects and talking to them on the phone but less success in closing sales then this would lead you to realise that you have an opportunity to improve your objection handling, presenting and closing skills. On the other hand, you may find that you are not particularly adept at handling the gatekeepers and getting through to customers but you are very skilled at qualifying them and closing the order.

4. DEALING WITH REJECTION

Having clear goals and activity goals in particular, helps us deal systematically with the problem of rejection. By keeping focused on making the calls and hitting our activity goals we can make sure that we do not get side-tracked by having a succession of minor defeats. The very essence of selling by telephone is the large number of calls you can take or make in a short period of time. By its very nature this involves a great deal of rejection. It is important, however, to remember that the customer or prospect is not rejecting you. When the customer says 'no' what they really mean is not today. By setting ourselves a clear activity goal of say 100 calls a day we can give ourselves a sense of achievement by knowing that we have made this number of calls, even if on that particular day the calls have been relatively unproductive. Remember the only failure in selling by telephone is not getting failure in the call but not making the calls in the first place.

5. FILLING THE FUNNEL

Prospecting, cold-calling, or warm calling are all activities which are know as filling the funnel. In order to put a certain number of sales on the board it is essential to do a certain number of calls. The trick with filling the funnel is to make sure that it is done consistently. Otherwise a roller coaster effect can happen. This issue is covered in more detail on page 76.

Voice projection

As well as identifying your sources of good prospects and having a planned approach to working the list, time also needs to be taken in how you project your voice. If you were selling face-to-face your impression will be created very much by how you looked, dressed and behaved when in front of the potential prospect or customer. This is why, for example, many customer service and sales staff that work in a retail environment are given uniforms or standards of dress they have to meet. As well as presenting a uniform image, it also ensures that a positive impression is made in the mind of the customer. When we are working on the telephone it is diffi-cult to put on a uniform with our voice, but we do have to make a very positive impression using primarily voice tone and the words we use in order to impress the customer.

Record yourself on a telephone call and then play it back and listen to yourself and ask yourself if you are creating a positive impres-sion, how good do you sound on the telephone, do you sound confident, friendly, helpful, efficient and so on.

Smile when you dial

A smile can actually be heard down the telephone. With a practised ear it is possible to hear when somebody is smiling, standing up, sitting down, or slouched and depressed when they are talking on the telephone. The underlying point to this is that a smile can actually be the same as a handshake, a smile and eye contact when you are meeting somebody face-to-face. When we meet or greet somebody for the first time, we always need to classify them as whether they are friend or foe, an instinct that goes back many centuries. By putting a smile in our voice we instantly alert the customer that we mean them well. Of course what we really mean is to sell them something, but then again you are only doing this to provide a service and to help them.

Project a winning voice tone

The voice tone is how we look on the telephone. It is controlled by such things as the speed of our speech, the clarity of how we talk, the pace of our words and the volume. Pitch is also very important, that is, how we enunciate words, or vary our voice tone to make it sound more interesting. Have you ever been talking to somebody on the telephone who speaks in a complete monotone? You probably find it very difficult to maintain a positive impression or even to keep your attention. Take a few moments to make some notes on how your voice sounds, and how you think you can improve it. Also identify people who you think have a very good telephone voice and what it is that makes them sound so impressive.

Have excellent product knowledge

Product knowledge is essential in selling, and is especially important when selling on the telephone. It conveys confidence, credibility and allows you to truly add value to what is being sold by allowing you to advise the customer well in advance what it is they want to buy.

It is very unlikely that a customer will want to proceed with a purchase without having certain questions answered. These may be technical or trivial but they all carry equal importance. One advantage of working over the telephone is that you can, of course, have product information immediately to hand so that if somebody were to ask you technical or detailed price information you could look it up on a chart or a booklet in front of you. However, do not rely on this advantage.

> Have all brochures, catalogues, manuals etc, to hand when making a sales call.

It is important that you take time on a regular basis to invest in product knowledge. This means not only knowing the features of your product or service, but what these features do, their advantages to the customer and ultimately the benefit to the customer. *The two keys to selling successfully over the telephone are enthusiasm and benefits.* Benefits really require a sound understanding of your products and service and how it relates to your customer.

The sales call

Good first impressions are essential.

How you open the call, that is the very first initial greeting and statements and questions, can play a large part in how the call develops. It has been said that in the first few minutes of meeting people face-to-face we make our mind up about them very quickly. This is twice as true when using the telephone.

If you are making an outgoing call for example, chances are that you will have interrupted the other person whilst they were doing something else. People do not sit around waiting for the telephone to ring hoping that it is a sales person that might have a special offer for them. They are usually busy doing other things. It is therefore important that you make your opening very succinct clear and friendly.

Essentials

- Clear greeting: 'Good morning'
- Your company or organisation name – pronounced clearly and slowly
- Your name
- An offer of help: 'How can I help you?'

After listening carefully to the customer's initial reason for calling – ask for their name and repeat yours. This will make the call more personal and may help you to keep control.

The voice that sells

The three V's

Spoken sales messages are comprised of three components:

Verbal – the words we speak, which is our message.

Vocal – the way in which we say the words.

Visual – the image people form when we say the words.

As you know, the *believability* of a message is based on these percentages: verbal, seven per cent; vocal, 38 per cent; visual, 55 per cent.

Therefore, because the phone is a non-visual medium, 93 per cent of a message's believability (vocal's 38 per cent plus visual's 55 per cent) is communicated by the *way* the message is presented – that is, *how* you sound.

Ways to improve the way you sound

ARTICULATION

Listen to your calls on tape and define any problem areas.

Recite tongue twisters: slowly at first, then speed up until you make no mistakes. Here are some examples:

'The tip of the tongue, the lips, and the teeth.'

'Rubber baby buggy bumpers.'

INFLECTION

Listen again to the taped calls for any problem areas.

Select an article from a magazine and read into the tape recorder, varying your voice dramatically.

RATE OF SPEECH

Adjust your rate of speech slightly. If necessary speak more deliberately and slowly, to match that of the person you are calling.

VOLUME

Speak as if you were talking to a person across a desk from you. Deepen your voice for more credibility.

PAUSING

For impact, pause at areas other than where periods and commas would normally appear.

DRAMATIC VARIATION

Raise your voice, and lower it to make a point.

BODY LANGUAGE

Sit up straight or stand up.

Talk to a person.

Close your eyes and visualise the other person.

Think quickly, talk slowly.

Telephone sales questioning techniques

Sales questioning on the telephone is comprised of ten inter-locking methods or skills. These are:

1. **Attending** – small noises and acknowledgements – 'aha', 'yes', 'I see'

2. **Reflection** – repeating the last words of a prospect's statement

3. **Selective reflection** – repeating a selected word(s) from prospect's statement

4. **Open questions** – asking questions that will not get a *yes/no* answer

5. **Closed questions** – asking questions that look for confirmation

6. **High-impact questions** – asking questions that get the customer to evaluate, speculate or analyse

7. **Testing understanding** – repeating back in your own words what you think the other person has said

8. **Linking phrases** – using phrases that move you naturally from one topic to another or move you further into the same topic

9. **Summarising** – repeating what has been agreed

10. **Silence** – avoiding interrupting when prospect is speaking, or jumping in and answering your own questions before prospect has had time to reply.

Customers
must be
listened to,
before they will
listen to you.

Here is a summary of each skill area:

ATTENDING

Attending behaviour means that you give your prospect your complete attention. The prospect must be able to hear and feel that you are listening attentively by your verbal behaviour ie acknowledgements, questions, encouraging noises, etc.

Attending helps your prospect feel free to say whatever is important to them. They will feel that you are listening and concerned. Attending makes listening possible.

Attending is a subtle and intense activity. It is difficult to describe how to attend. However, one important point is not concentrating on acting as if you are giving attention.

The way to go about attending is to concentrate on your prospect, listening to what is being said and using your voice to show you are listening. The effect of this will be to transmit to the prospect that you are giving all of your attention.

REFLECTION

The salesperson simply echoes back to the prospect the last words or word the prospect said before pausing. Or the salesperson may rephrase the last few words, expressing the same meaning as the prospect but in different words. Reflection is then either literal or rephrased. It is a way of conveying that the salesperson is paying attention, is interested, and above all, prompts the prospect to continue in a way that the salesperson feels is meaningful. It is a technique that invites the prospect to reveal thoughts. A direct question takes the prospect in a certain direction, so that options for developing a theme are restricted.

A combination of reflection and attending is a pure and simple method of *drawing* out.

Example:

Prospect: 'I am thinking of taking a new line of stock.'

Salesperson: 'New stock?'

Prospect: 'Yes, we want to offer a more comprehensive service.'

SELECTIVE REFLECTION

Reflection echoes the last few words that have been said. Selective reflection picks out, from a whole body of statements, a few words or phrases that carry a suppressed meaning. Examples are phrases that are accompanied by noticeable non-verbal agitation or phrases that appear to be impromptu asides or slips of the tongue. These words or phrases are simply echoed back literally to the prospect.

Example:

Prospect: 'Well, I'm finding our present supplier a little *difficult* at the moment.'

Salesperson: 'A little *difficult*?'

Prospect: 'Yes, they are not giving the service we look for.'

OPEN QUESTIONS

These questions invite the prospect to give more than a yes/no answer. If used properly, they stimulate information giving and avoid the interview becoming an interrogation. Open questions begin with the words:

- HOW?
- WHAT?
- WHY?
- WHEN?
- WHERE?
- WHO?

When you ask open questions you have to give the prospect time to answer ie when you ask the question remain silent, wait for the answer. Remember the prospect has to think in order to reply. Don't let the silence force you into letting them 'off the hook'.

Example:

Salesperson: 'What made you choose your present supplier?'

Prospect: (Thinking about reply.)

Salesperson: (Before prospect has replied) 'Was it the cost or service provided?'

Here the salesperson has jumped in before the prospect has had a chance to answer. Remember, when you ask an open question **WAIT** (use silence) for the answer. Open questions should be used to gain information.

CLOSED QUESTIONS

These questions invite the prospect to give a yes/no answer and should therefore be avoided when you are looking for information as you have to ask a lot of them. Alternatively, closed questions can cause you to assume (ie if you ask a closed question intending to get information, you have **ASSUMED** the answer before formulating the question).

Example:

Salesperson: 'Do you have a security system on the machines?'

Prospect: 'No we don't.'

Salesperson: 'Does that cause you a problem?'

Prospect: 'No.'

Salesperson: 'Aren't you worried about fraud?'

Prospect: 'No, I keep the machine in my safe.'

We usually fall into this trap because we are trying to 'force-fit' the features of our products before we understand the prospect's needs.

Closed questions are essential in selling, they begin with the words:

- **DO YOU...**
- **HAVE YOU...**
- **ARE YOU...**
- **IS IT...**
- **HAVE THEY...**

etc.

Closed questions should be used to get **CONFIRMATION** when testing understanding or summarising.

Example (summarising):

Salesperson: 'So far we have agreed that...

...you need a faster system

...good security

...and a system that can be maintained easily.

Is that correct?'

Answers to closed questions can also mislead us.

Example:

Salesperson: 'Is your system reliable?'

Prospect: 'Yes it is'

Here prospects can easily get rid of this line of questioning if they want to, even if their system is not totally reliable.

Remember – ask closed questions for confirmation.

Avoid using them to gain information as they can **MISLEAD** or make you **ASSUME**.

HIGH-IMPACT QUESTIONS

High-impact questions maximise the sales call by returning high-value information in an efficient amount of time.

High-impact questions = high value information.

High-impact questions require customers to think, organise information, and search for new meanings to existing information before responding. They ask customers to:

- evaluate or analyse
- speculate
- express feelings
- react.

The result is the type of information you might hear if you were to attend a customer's problem-solving or planning session. Good high-impact questions make customers say:

- '...I don't know. I never thought about that.'
- 'Hmm... I never put those ideas together that way before.'

High-impact questions should be:

- brief and clear
- open-ended
- phrased to require a thoughtful answer
- relevant to the customer's situation and position.

Using high-impact questions in sales calls has several benefits to you. High-impact questions are likely to:

- involve the customer by requiring him or her to think
- increase the amount of time that customers talk
- provide new insights into problems
- produce high-quality information
- expose underlying issues
- result in telesales-people being seen as perceptive professionals who can function as consultants
- cause the customer to believe that the sales call was valuable.

High-impact and open-ended questions: a comparison

Open-ended questions invite customers to respond with more than a yes or no answer. However, open-ended questions may elicit factual information that easily could be found in files, Annual Reports, or organisational charts, or are well-known and easy to answer.

Customers who enjoy talking about their organisations or themselves may respond willingly to open-ended questions for a while, since it allows them to talk. However, such conversation usually does not require customers to engage in high-level thinking, nor is it likely to produce any new insights of value for them.

Tips on high-impact questions:

- Prepare high-impact questions to use with a customer as part of your sales tool kit.

- Once in front of a customer, you may use these prepared questions or devise others spontaneously in response to points the customer has raised.

Encourage the customer

High-impact questions are tough to answer. The customer may feel interrogated. By encouraging frequently, you can take the edge off your high-impact questions and make the section more conversational.

High-impact question examples: evaluate or analyse:

- How would you compare X to Y?

- How do you plan to evaluate this?

- What are the three most important difficulties you face in...?

Speculate

- What does the trend in… mean to you?
- If you could improve your current supplier, what would it be?
- How do you see your requirements changing in the future?

Express feelings

You have said that attracting new customers is important. What else do you feel is important to your establishment's growth over the next two years?

- How do you feel…?
- What are feelings towards?
- What do you feel is most important with regards to…?

React(ive)

- How will the new tax laws impact your current fleet costs?
- How will the recent drop in ticket prices impact your company's profit picture? You'll hopefully have more passengers, but how profitable will they be?

Asking difficult questions

Introduction

- Some questions may be challenging to ask because they are personal, controversial, or direct in nature. One way to ask difficult questions is with the supported question format.
- Reason + benefit + question.

Supported questions

- A supported question braces a difficult question with the reason for the question and the benefit to the customer of responding. This format helps you to earn the right to ask the difficult question.

Example:

- 'Let's ensure that we include everyone from your company that needs to be involved.' (*reason*)

- 'This will enable you to provide any necessary information to them up front and to reduce the need for repetition.' (*benefit*)

- 'Who in your company would be responsible for making this type of decision?' (*question*)

TESTING UNDERSTANDING

In testing understanding, the salesperson repeats back in their own words what the prospect has just said. This technique emphasises listening and helps reduce misunderstanding.

Example:

Prospect: 'We are quite happy with our present service.'

Salesperson: 'Are you saying you don't see any advantages to a lower priced/faster/more secure system?'

Prospect: 'Not exactly. You see...'

In using this technique we:

1. check to make sure we understand what the prospect means

2. give evidence to the prospect that we understand the spirit and feelings underlying what the prospect is saying

3. invite the prospect to go on and give more information.

LINKING PHRASES

Linking phrases help the sales process move naturally from one topic to another or deeper into the same topic. They help reduce the 'interrogation syndrome' which often characterises information gathering calls where salespeople ask one question after another.

Linking phrases help make the call conversational and friendly.

Examples of linking phrases:

- Tell me about your business...
- Future plans
- Structure
- Present method, etc
- That's interesting, what other problems does it cause?
- What's the effect, etc
- I can understand how
- What was the effect... you feel
- Let me just summarise
- I feel we've agreed...
- Can I just ask you a question here?
- What do you...
- Are you saying... You don't like, etc
- You sound upset about your present supply situation, etc.

SUMMARISING

In summarising, the salesperson repeats back information that has been agreed. As with testing understanding, it shows you have been listening and helps reduce misunderstanding.

Example:

Salesperson: 'So far we have agreed that you need overnight delivery of supplies system and reduce stationery costs, is that right?'

Remember, summarising should be carried out throughout the call, not just at the review stage.

SILENCE

Silence is one of the most powerful techniques for eliciting information from others.

Silence creates pressure (on both parties).

Good communicators learn to use silence at the appropriate time to draw the prospect out and to avoid jumping in and answering their own questions.

Key times to use silence are:

1. just after the prospect has finished talking
2. when you have asked an open question
3. when you have closed for commitment
4. whilst the prospect is talking.

1	A pause after the prospect has finished talking will often elicit more information.

Example:

Prospect: '...and finally, I'm not happy with the present system'

Salesperson: SILENT

Prospect: 'It's always breaking down...'

2	When you have asked an open question always give the prospect time to think and answer.

Example:

Salesperson: 'Why did you choose your present system?'

Prospect: (Thinking)

Prospect: 'Because it offered selection and was easy to use.'

3	When you have closed for commitment always wait for a yes (or no); if you jump in you may talk yourself out of a sale.

Example (*wrong*):

Salesperson: 'As you have agreed, this new machine will... (summarise benefits), shall we go ahead?'

Prospect: (Thinking.)

Salesperson: 'Or would you like to think some more?'

(not using silence)

Prospect: 'Yes please.'

| **4** | Avoid interrupting whilst the prospect is talking. If you want to intervene use a linking phrase (such as 'Can I just |

see if we understood what you've said' to test for understanding); in this way the prospect will feel you are trying to listen. Once you've got control you can change direction if you want to.

Example:

Prospect: Talk Talk Talk

Salesperson: 'Let me see if I've got this right. Do you mean...?'

Prospect: 'Yes, we're fed up with them.'

Salesperson: 'Then let me ask you a question. What would you look for in...?'

Features and benefits (FAB)

Sell the sizzle... not the sausage!

A customer or prospect's **needs and wants** have to be fulfilled if the sale is to be successful. So, however skilled you are as a telephone salesperson in questioning and uncovering needs, the prospect will be unlikely to purchase until he is satisfied that your product/service will meet his needs. Therefore during a telephone call, or several other calls, the salesperson will have to give the customer information about their products.

Many telesales-people fall into the trap of talking about their product/service before they understand what the prospect is looking for specifically. This leads to the prospect raising objections and reduces the chances of a sale.

Prospects buy when they recognise that the needs they have can be matched by the benefit that your products can offer.

Some ways of describing your products to your customers are more persuasive than others and therefore the chances of making a sale will be increased. It is essential that we have a clear understanding of the definition of *Feature, Advantage* and *Benefit*, so that we are aware of the degree of persuasiveness each represents. Bear in mind that prospects buy what your product or service will do for them, not what it is.

For the best effect only mention features and benefits that are relevant and personalised.

Feature statement. Facts

A feature is a statement made by the salesperson which relates directly to the characteristics of a product and can usually be answered by the question 'What is it?'

As a feature statement has little meaning on its own, it usually has little effect on the customer.

Advantage statement. Functions

An advantage statement describes what the product feature does or how it can help the prospect.

As advantage statements expand on the feature and explain what the feature means and what it will do, then it is apparent that an advantage statement is going to be somewhat more persuasive than a feature statement.

However, people buy because of the benefits which they will derive from your product in answer to their needs.

So what is a benefit? Value

A benefit statement is an advantage statement which is related directly to a pre-stated need of the customer and answers the specific question 'What will it do for me?'

Link statements with phrases such as 'Which means that', 'Therefore...'

We must always remember 'telling isn't selling'. Before we begin to discuss our solution, therefore, we must first determine what it is the prospect wants and for what reasons. Before we tell a customer all about our solution we should first ask the questions 'Does he really need to know this? Is it going to be of interest to him?' Do both of you have an understanding of the prospect's clear needs?

Developing FAB statements

Remember five of the most common buying motives a customer may have is a desire to either:

- **increase something**
- **improve something**
- **reduce or decrease something**
- **save something or**
- **gain something.**

Examples – fleet servicing contract

FEATURE	BENEFIT
Free pick-up and collect of all vehicles from your offices	• *Save time* • *Reduced hassle* • *Easy and convenient*
Fully itemised monthly invoices	• *Improved reconciliation* • *Saves time in the accounts department*
Volume discount prices on tyres	• *Saves money and time in shopping around for prices*
Free valet and wash on all vehicles	• *Improved satisfaction with service by drivers*

People buy for different reasons

People buy largely for a combination of two factors:

1. Emotional and subjective reasons (largely unconscious).

2. Tangible and logical reasons (conscious).

For example, consider the elements in choosing a mobile phone – a product commonly purchased over the telephone:

Mobile phone

Emotional and subjective reasons for buying (largely unconscious)

- Brand name
- What will my friends say?
- Does it look good?
- What will it say about me?
- Is it the right image?
- Peace of mind in case of faults?
- Colour
- Do I *like* the person selling it to me?
- Do I trust them?

Tangible and logical reasons for buying (conscious)

- Service coverage
- Is it in my budget?
- Is it easy to use?
- Does it have the right functions?
- Size
- Has it been reviewed favourably in the magazines?

> To increase buying desire find out 'want'. Highlight or discuss how they will gain or benefit from fulfilling this want.

Matching

The objective of matching is to match what you are recommending to what the customer wants.

You must establish what the customer needs in order to know what to sell him. Don't try to sell until you know what the customer wants.

Needs are individual and it is the telesales person's job to establish what they are in each case. The customer may not always realise that the need exists, in which case the telesales person should point out a need first. Having found the need he/she can show how the customer will satisfy the need by agreeing to an appointment or sale.

Matching without need is an uphill task. Needs provide information to buy. Don't sell the product or service until you know what the customer wants.

Don't tell the customer what your service is. Tell him/her what it will do for them.

What makes one service better than another, it is not that it has more features or benefits, but that it does more of what the customer wants it to.

At this point you must be certain to know those aspects of your organisation which can be of benefit to the customer so that you can choose those which relate directly to him/her to take the appointment or sales.

Use your imagination to adapt the selling points to each
case to make the match as accurate as possible. Make
sure that he/she understands and is convinced of how
each point will benefit him and his business.

Remember that very few services are so good that they sell
themselves, and the knowledge and sheer enthusiasm with which
you present is all important. Give your matching a structure so that
it has a logical sequence and works toward a conclusion.

Selling benefits that need both emotional and logical needs

A single feature can often have many different benefits. Some of
these might be logical and very tangible, others more subjective.
For example, in the above illustration, what could be the possible
practical benefit of having a mobile phone that would allow you
to change the colour to suit your mood or outfit? It certainly won't
improve your line quality or reduce your call charges.

Because of the lack of visual communication on the telephone it is
vital the benefits are explained and mentioned well and clearly.

*People don't buy a product or service...
they buy how they imagine they will feel
using the product or service.*

Handling objections and questions

Handling customer objections

When you are asked a question about a feature or benefit, don't jump in with a specific answer until you know what it is you are answering. Use the structure below for answering questions. In summary, it is possible to answer a question in three ways:

1. by giving information only

2. with a question only

3. by giving information followed by a question.

It is best to employ No. 3 where possible in order to regain control, and find out why the customer is asking the question.

Objections fall into two categories:

Real and **Insincere**

There are two types of real objections:

- **Genuine objections**

- **Misunderstandings**

Insincere objections take the form of **EXCUSES.**

WHY DO REAL OBJECTIONS OCCUR?

Most real objections occur when salespeople offer 'solutions' that the customer does not consider relevant. Thus many objections are the product of a **misunderstanding** or **mismatch.**

This situation usually occurs when salespeople assume needs or react to vague needs. They offer solutions without fully developing clear needs by asking problem effect and commitment questions.

Because the salesperson does not understand the clear need, they will probably offer the wrong solution or a partial solution which the customer will reject.

Objections also occur because your product/service has a genuine disadvantage to that of your competitor(s). These are hardest to deal with and have to be outweighed by emphasising the benefits of your product/service which can only be done if you have a good understanding of the customer's clear need. Therefore, sound need creation is the secret to avoiding **misunderstandings** and answering **genuine** objections.

Insincere objections or excuses occur when 'political' situations exist or when you are talking to the wrong person, and should be identified by asking the customer if they will commit if you can prove to their satisfaction that you can handle their objections. This technique is known as **confirming**.

How *not* to overcome objections

When faced with an objection there are several traps to avoid falling into.

ARGUING/JUSTIFYING

We often see an objection as a personal attack and consequently argue/defend the situation. The problem with this is:

- if you win the argument you lose the customer. If you lose the argument you still lose the customer, or

- if you start to justify, you are saying to the customer: 'You are right.'

EXAGGERATING

It is easy to exaggerate product/service capabilities when faced with an objection. This will only lead to future problems when the customer finds out your product won't do what you said it would.

REPLYING TOO QUICKLY

If you jump in too quickly you may answer what is not really an objection or the answer you give may appear too glib.

AGREEING

If you agree with an objection you have to put in the word 'but' (ie 'Yes… but'), which is always seen as a disagreement.

For example:

Customer: 'You're very expensive.'

Salesperson: 'Yes, we are, but…'

IGNORING

Ignoring an objection can be dangerous. If the customer thinks it is important he will expect you to answer it: if you don't, he may assume you are hiding something.

DEFERRING

You will probably have deduced from what has been covered that objections can only be handled effectively if the salesperson has a sound understanding of the broker's situation and where the product or service will solve problems.

Very often, however, objections occur early in the sale before the salesperson has been able to develop clear needs; in this situation the salesperson should defer the objection rather than try to answer it. This is necessary because the salesperson will not be able to handle the objection because he doesn't have enough information about the customer situation, ie the problems, buying criteria, future requirements etc. If the salesperson attempts to handle the early objection he runs the risk of losing control, and the sale, because the arguments will be weak through lack of information.

When **deferring**, the salesperson should acknowledge the objection and move it to a point further into the sale when there is enough information to handle it.

For example:

Customer *(at start of call)*: 'Your rates are not competitive enough for us.'

Salesperson deferring: 'May I come back to our rates in a moment, first may I ask what...?'

Overcoming objections

Sequence overview

When dealing with objections the first stage is to handle the objection and secondly to then answer it. Most salespeople feel more comfortable using their own words rather than using a script.

- <PAUSE>
- **Clarify and isolate**
- **Listen**
- **Evaluate**
- **Answer with a benefit or negotiate a solution**
- **Review and re-cap.**

You'll notice that the first step when dealing with an objection is to clarify. It is also prudent to wait a few seconds before answering an objection.

The pause

  a. Gives us time to think.

  b. Shows the customer we are thinking about it.

  c. The customer may give more information or even answer it themselves.

Therefore, on hearing an objection, having **paused** we need to **refine** it into something which is more understandable.

The next stage is to determine that this objection is the only one. You don't want to handle it and then get another immediately. This stage is called **clarifying** and **isolating**.

Clarify

'I'm surprised you say that, Mr Customer. What do you mean by…?'

Isolate

'Is this your only concern?'

Having isolated the objection we are now at the stage of determining whether the objection is real or an excuse. To establish the reason we need to confirm the objection and the customer's sincerity.

Listen

Show that you have heard and understood the objection by active listening, nodding, encouraging, summarising and rephrasing.

Evaluate

Is the objection due to a:

- misunderstanding
- missed need
- genuine concern
- excuse or insecurity
- minor point or major issue.

So whether the objection is a misunderstanding or whether it is genuine, both can be answered in the way suggested below:

Answer with a benefit or a concession.

Type of objection	How to answer
a. Genuine	• Maximise the benefits – paint the big picture • Minimise the objections • Trade or agree concession or change
b. Misunderstanding	• Re-explain FAB (Features and Benefits) • Probe for exact questions

With both these situations the next step is to check whether the customer's concern has been satisfied.

Review

Genuine or misunderstanding – **ALWAYS CHECK**.

'Does this now satisfy your concern?'

If the customer says 'No' – you would find out why.

If you tried to close the sale while he or she is still dissatisfied then it would be an obvious rejection.

Only if the customer said 'Yes', would you close the sale:

'Does this satisfy your concern?'

'Yes, it does.'

'In that case, shall we go ahead?' (Close)

Closing the sale

Most telesales-people's understanding of closing the sale is that it takes place at the end of a sales call. This is true, but salespeople who leave it until the end usually have to work harder at getting a decision from a customer.

Closing is a skill which should be displayed by salespeople throughout the call in terms of commitment, so that finally it doesn't come as a bolt out of the blue, but is natural, based upon the customer's earlier commitments.

What is a close?

A close is any question asked by the salesperson during a telesales call, which asks the customer to give commitment not just for the order but for commitment of interest.

Why don't salespeople close?

The reasons why salespeople don't close usually fall into the following categories:

1. They are frightened of rejection by the customer.
2. They are concerned not to offend the customer.
3. They can't recognise the moment.
4. They don't know how to close.

Throughout a sale you should be alert to your customer's signals, be it in the form of a question, or an agreement. Recognise and take advantage of the opportunities as they arise.

What should a closing question be?

The way in which you put your words together throughout selling is important, but none more so than when you are closing.

A good closing question is one which is positive in assumption and offers an alternative.

Closing questions can be asked at any time throughout the sale, but when it comes to the final close a structured approach is well worth adopting. When you have gained all the information you require in terms of customer needs and you are ready to discuss what your product will do related to what the customer wants, then use the following structure:

1. Summarise the agreed customer needs.
2. Relate the product advantages to the expressed customer needs (ie benefits).
3. Ask a closing question.

There are several main types of closing question and many different methods for closing the sale; the following will give you some idea. Remember to use one at a time, and practise using a number of them until you have perfected them (some will suit your personality and some won't, similarly, some will suit different circumstances), and use them accordingly.

Remember the three golden rules when closing:

1. A close must always be in the form of a question.

2. If you don't ask you don't get.

3. When you've asked a closing question, wait for the answer.

You won't be able to convert every sales enquiry or telephone call to an order, but be sure to leave the door open if you're unsuccessful. You never know when the customer will require your products in the future.

More sales are lost at the closing stages than at any other in the sales plan – often because the salesperson does not know what to say. Even when the techniques are known to them, they will frequently still hesitate – just through the feat of being turned down.

BE AWARE OF BUYING SIGNALS

These signals may be verbal or physical – any time the prospect indicates approval, or agreement with what you are saying.

Most people simply need firm reassurance that they are making a sound decision.

WHEN YOU GET A BUYING SIGNAL – ASK A CLOSING QUESTION

These are questions to which a positive answer commits them to buying from you.

- When you have asked a closing question – wait for the answer.

- Wait for however long it takes – there is pressure in silence.

Your relationship will not suffer by asking them to buy – because they know you are there to sell and they expect you to ask.

You need to be tough-minded about closing. This does not mean being overbearing or hard-boiled or using high pressure tactics.

Examples of closing questions

THE DIRECT QUESTION

Ask a closed question which requires a yes/no answer: 'Would you like to order this one?' You may get a no, if so, ask the customer why or what other product he or she would prefer.

THE ALTERNATIVE QUESTION

Give the customer alternatives from which to choose, eg 'Would you prefer to start on X or Y?'

THE SECONDARY QUESTION

Ask for a minor decision which paradoxically supersedes the major one. Ask your customer a question by which, in answering, he or she has transcended the major decision area and has in fact bought, eg 'Can we have your go-ahead, and who would you want to be trained on the machine?'

SHARP ANGLE

When your customer enquires about a certain aspect of your product or service, do not answer their question directly. Ask them whether or not he or she will have it. Use a little diplomacy, eg: 'When can you get the order faxed to us?'

Ending the call

Confirm agreement

- **Closed questions to summarise**
- **Restate to show understanding**
- **Clarify details**
- **Repeat your name/number**
- **Thank for time.**

Summarise the conversation, especially the actions to be taken.

- Thank the person for the call and time
- Hang up after the customer hangs up.

Plus

- Restate to show understanding
- Repeat your name and number
- Thank the person for their time.

The elements of effective openings reflect effective telephone practices.

End on a positive; 'Thank you for your order' and 'Look forward to talking to you again'.

Now let us consider the actual telephone call itself, whether this is incoming or outgoing, a customer call or an internal call.

In order for us to prepare, and therefore be more effective in our telephone selling, we need to consider the different types of call that we receive or make.

Most of your business calls will probably be a mixture of sales, service, information and problem-solving calls. When a call comes in, there is a good chance that it will be in the nature of a service or problem solving. If you are working in customer service most of the calls you place will most likely deal with service and information providing.

However, it is important for you to realise that while you might have a single purpose in mind when you take or make your call, your customer may change the nature of the call (eg problem solving). You must be prepared to handle all of these areas.

Telephone selling – application assignments

The following exercises will help you transfer the skills and methods from this section into your work.

1. Make a checklist of at least ten things that you would listen for when you are enquiring or buying on the telephone. Include whatever is important to you. Make sure each item is specific and measurable. For example, instead of 'asked questions', try 'asked open questions early in the call'.

2. Using a local or national newspaper or magazine, telephone five companies to enquire on their products or services. Mark each one using your checklist. Make a note of anything else you notice and decide the best and worst call.

3. Keep a file or cassette tape of 'sold well' and 'sold poorly' when buying on the telephone yourself.

4. Disguise your voice if you have to and make some 'mystery' shopper calls to your own company. Record the calls if possible and review with your team or colleagues.

5. Repeat the exercise above for some competitors. Make a relative comparison.

Thorogood publishing

Thorogood publishes a wide range of books, reports, special briefings and psychometric tests. Listed below is a selection of key titles.

Desktop Guides

The marketing strategy desktop guide	Norton Paley • £16.99	
The sales manager's desktop guide		
	Mike Gale and Julian Clay • £16.99	
The company director's desktop guide	David Martin • £16.99	
The credit controller's desktop guide	Roger Mason • £16.99	
The company secretary's desktop guide	Roger Mason • £16.99	
The finance and accountancy desktop guide	Ralph Tiffin • £16.99	
The commercial engineer's desktop guide	Tim Boyce • £16.99	
The training manager's desktop guide	Eddie Davies • £16.99	
The PR practitioner's desktop guide	Caroline Black • £16.99	
Win new business – the desktop guide	Susan Croft • £16.99	

Masters in Management

Mastering business planning and strategy	Paul Elkin • £14.99
Mastering financial management	Stephen Brookson • £14.99
Mastering leadership	Michael Williams • £14.99
Mastering negotiations	Eric Evans • £14.99
Mastering people management	Mark Thomas • £14.99
Mastering personal and interpersonal skills	
	Peter Haddon • £14.99
Mastering project management	Cathy Lake • £14.99
Mastering marketing	Ian Ruskin-Brown • £16.99

Business Action Pocketbooks

Edited by David Irwin

Building your business pocketbook	£6.99
Developing yourself and your staff pocketbook	£6.99
Finance and profitability pocketbook	£6.99
Managing and employing people pocketbook	£6.99
Sales and marketing pocketbook	£6.99

Managing projects and operations pocketbook	£6.99
Effective business communications pocketbook	£6.99
PR techniques that work	*Edited by Jim Dunn* • £6.99

Other titles

The John Adair handbook of management and leadership	*Edited by Neil Thomas* • £24.99
The pension trustee's handbook (3rd edition)	*Robin Ellison* • £25
Boost your company's profits	*Barrie Pearson* • £12.99
Negotiate to succeed	*Julie Lewthwaite* • £12.99
The management tool kit	*Sultan Kermally* • £10.99
Working smarter	*Graham Roberts-Phelps* • £14.99
Test your management skills	*Michael Williams* • £15.99
The art of headless chicken management	*Elly Brewer and Mark Edwards* • £6.99
EMU challenge and change – the implications for business	*John Atkin* • £11.99
Everything you need for an NVQ in management	*Julie Lewthwaite* • £22.99
Customer relationship management	*Graham Roberts-Phelps* • £14.99
Sales management and organisation	*Peter Green* • £10.99
Telephone tactics	*Graham Roberts-Phelps* • £10.99
Companies don't succeed people do!	*Graham Roberts-Phelps* • £12.99
Inspiring leadership	*John Adair* • £15.99
The book of ME	*Barrie Pearson and Neil Thomas* • £14.99
The complete guide to debt recovery	*Roger Mason* • £12.99
Janner's complete speechmaker	*Greville Janner* • £10.99
Gurus on business strategy	*Tony Grundy* • £14.99
Dynamic practice development	*Kim Tasso* • £19.99
Successful selling solutions	*Julian Clay* • £12.99
High performance consulting skills	*Mark Thomas* • £14.99
The concise Adair on leadership	*edited by Neil Thomas* • £9.99
The inside track to successful management	*Gerry Kushel* • £12.99

The concise time management and personal development	*John Adair and Melanie Allen* • £9.99
Gurus on marketing	*Sultan Kermally* • £14.99
The concise Adair on communication and presentation skills	*edited by Neil Thomas* • £9.99
The dictionary of colour	*Ian Paterson* • £19.99

Thorogood also has an extensive range of reports and special briefings which are written specifically for professionals wanting expert information.

For a full listing of all Thorogood publications, or to order any title, please call Thorogood Customer Services on 020 7749 4748 or fax on 020 7729 6110. Alternatively view our website at www.thorogood.ws.

Focused on developing your potential

Falconbury, sister company to Thorogood publishing, brings together the leading experts from all areas of management and strategic development to provide you with a comprehensive portfolio of action-centred training and learning.

We understand everything managers and leaders need to **be, know and do** to succeed in today's commercial environment. Each product addresses a different technical or personal development need that will encourage growth and increase your potential for success.

* Practical public training programmes
* Tailored in-company training
* Coaching
* Mentoring
* Topical business seminars
* Trainer bureau/bank
* Adair Leadership Foundation

The most valuable resource in any organisation is its people; it is essential that you invest in the development of your management and leadership skills to ensure your team fulfil their potential. Investment into both personal and professional development has been proven to provide an outstanding ROI through increased productivity in both you and your team. Ultimately leading to a dramatic impact on the bottom line.

With this in mind Falconbury have developed a comprehensive portfolio of training programmes to enable managers of all levels to develop their skills in leadership, communications, finance, people management, change management and all areas vital to achieving success in today's commercial environment.

What Falconbury can offer you?

- Practical applied methodology with a proven results
- Extensive bank of experienced trainers
- Limited attendees to ensure one-to-one guidance
- Up to the minute thinking on management and leadership techniques
- Interactive training
- Balanced mix of theoretical and practical learning
- Learner-centred training
- Excellent cost/quality ratio

Falconbury In-Company Training

Falconbury are aware that a public programme may not be the solution to leadership and management issues arising in your firm. Involving only attendees from your organisation and tailoring the programme to focus on the current challenges you face individually and as a business may be more appropriate. With this in mind we have brought together our most motivated and forward thinking trainers to deliver tailored in-company programmes developed specifically around the needs within your organisation.

All our trainers have a practical commercial background and highly refined people skills. During the course of the programme they act as facilitator, trainer and mentor, adapting their style to ensure that each individual benefits equally from their knowledge to develop new skills.

Falconbury works with each organisation to develop a programme of training that fits your needs, this can incorporate not only traditional class-room style learning but also involve our coaching and mentoring service or advise on the development of internal mentoring programmes.

Mentoring

Falconbury delivers a world class, individual mentoring service for senior executives and entrepreneurs. The purpose is to accelerate corporate success dramatically and to enhance personal development.

Mentoring involves formulating winning strategies, setting goals, mon-itoring achievements and motivating the whole team whilst achieving a much improved work life balance.

The issues are addressed at regular meetings, with telephone discussions in between. Sometimes, an unexpected issue will require an additional meeting at short notice.

Coaching

Developing and achieving your personal objectives in the workplace is becoming increasingly difficult in today's constantly changing environ-ment. Additionally, as a manager or leader, you are responsible for guiding colleagues towards the realisation of their goals. Sometimes it is easy to lose focus on your short and long-term aims.

Falconbury's one-to-one coaching draws out individual potential by raising self-awareness and understanding, facilitating the learning and perform-ance development that creates excellent managers and leaders. It builds renewed self-confidence and a strong sense of 'can-do' competence, contributing significant benefit to the organisation. Enabling you to focus your energy on developing your potential and that of your colleagues.

For more information on all our services please contact Falconbury on 020 7729 6677 or visit the website at: www.falconbury.co.uk